THIS BOOK BELONGS TO

_____

START DATE

_____

SHE READS TRUTH

FOUNDERS

FOUNDER
Raechel Myers

CO-FOUNDER
Amanda Bible Williams

EXECUTIVE

CHIEF EXECUTIVE OFFICER
Ryan Myers

EDITORIAL

MANAGING EDITOR
Lindsey Jacobi, MDiv

PRODUCTION EDITOR
Hannah Little, MTS

ASSOCIATE EDITOR
Kayla De La Torre, MAT

COPY EDITOR
Becca Owens, MA

CREATIVE

SENIOR ART DIRECTOR
Annie Glover

DESIGN MANAGER
Kelsea Allen

DESIGNERS
Savannah Ault
Ashley Phillips

MARKETING

MARKETING LEAD
Kelsey Chapman

PRODUCT MARKETING MANAGER
Krista Squibb

CONTENT MARKETING STRATEGIST
Tameshia Williams, ThM

SOCIAL MEDIA SPECIALIST
Bella Ponce

OPERATIONS

OPERATIONS DIRECTOR
Allison Sutton

COMMUNITY ENGAGEMENT

COMMUNITY ENGAGEMENT MANAGER
Delaney Coleman

COMMUNITY ENGAGEMENT SPECIALISTS
Cait Baggerman
Katy McKnight

SHIPPING

SHIPPING MANAGER
Marian Welch

FULFILLMENT LEAD
Hannah Song

FULFILLMENT SPECIALISTS
Bonnie Nickander
Kelsey Simpson

SUBSCRIPTION INQUIRIES
orders@shereadstruth.com

CONTRIBUTORS

PHOTOGRAPHY
Mia Grace Hardaway (162)

SPECIAL THANKS
Jessica Lamb, MA
Beth Joseph, MDiv
Oghosa Iyamu, MDiv
Bailey Gillespie
Jeremy Mitchell
Abbey Benson
Amanda Brush
Aimee Lindamood
Lauren Haag
Davis Camp DeLisi

SHE READS TRUTH™

© 2021, 2025 by She Reads Truth, LLC
All rights reserved. First edition 2021.
Second edition 2025.

All photography used by permission.

ISBN 978-1-962221-40-5

1 2 3 4 5 6 7 8 9 10

@SHEREADSTRUTH

 Download the She Reads Truth app, available for iOS and Android

Subscribe to the She Reads Truth Podcast

This book was printed offset in Nashville, Tennessee, on 70# Lynx Opaque. Cover is 100# Cougar Opaque with a soft touch lamination.

JOHN

SHE READS TRUTH

John's Gospel is an
open door into the
life-changing ministry
and message of Jesus.

Raechel Myers
FOUNDER

I have loved the music of Harry Connick Jr. for more than twenty years. "We Are in Love" has been our song since Ryan and I were dating in high school, and so many others have been the soundtrack to our story over the years. From "Lofty's Roach Soufflé" to "Bourbon Street Parade," Harry's musicianship has kept him at the tip-top of the list of concerts I'd love to one day attend.

For my birthday a few years back, my concert-going dream became a reality when Ryan surprised me with tickets to a Harry Connick Jr. show at an outdoor amphitheater just south of Nashville. We looked forward to it for months, but when the day finally arrived, a sudden-onset thunderstorm threatened to cancel the event altogether. We sat in our car outside the venue that night, waiting and hoping as the lightning crashed and the rain poured. More than an hour later, after the worst of the threat had passed and most of the concert goers had given up and headed home, we heard the update: "Harry wants to sing!" Braving the still-pouring rain, we ran from the car and found our seat among the remaining guests scattered sparsely throughout the amphitheater.

The opening number was spectacular, but it couldn't prepare us for what happened next. "Assigned seating is out the window tonight, folks!" Harry announced. "Come on down, and let's have a good time—I'm going to give you everything I've got!" Through the rain the remnant came, filing into seats we didn't pay for at a show we didn't think would happen, greeting each other with the same kindness we'd been shown by our generous host. In the middle of the storm, Harry beckoned us to "come and see" the good thing that was even better than we'd hoped it could be.

Friends, you hold in your hands a personal invitation to come and see Jesus—up close! John's Gospel tells the story of the life and ministry of Jesus Christ, showing Him to be the divine Son of God and compelling us to respond by putting our faith in Him. This Reading Guide will walk you through all twenty-one chapters over the course of five weeks, providing additional resources along the way to help you get the most from your reading. Take time to record your observations on the daily worksheet, and don't miss the other curated extras like the "Witnesses of Jesus" on page 118.

John's Gospel is an open door into the life-changing ministry and message of Jesus. We've all got seats we couldn't pay for if we tried—all the more reason to make room for strangers and friends to join us! So invite a friend, and settle in. Let's read the story of the Son of God, and let's be different because of it.

DESIGN ON PURPOSE

At She Reads Truth, we believe in pairing the inherently beautiful Word of God with the aesthetic beauty it deserves. Each of our resources is thoughtfully and artfully designed to highlight the beauty, goodness, and truth of Scripture in a way that reflects the themes of each curated reading plan.

For this book, we drew inspiration from the unique style of John's writing and his clear depiction of Christ as the Son of God. While the other three Gospels approach the story of Jesus from a more ministry-driven perspective, John emphasizes the identity of Jesus as God incarnate. The whimsical nature of the photos we used are a nod to John's poetic language, while the lines and layout remind us of the clarity with which he wrote about who Jesus is.

The colors used throughout the book point back to Christ: Gold, running as the main color throughout, reminds us of the glory of Jesus, the Word made flesh. And the off-white highlights His victory over the grave.

ANALOGUE

ABCDEFGHIJKLMN
OPQRSTUVWXYZ

REGULAR

abcdefghijklm
nopqrstuvwxyz

ITALIC

abcdefghijklm
nopqrstuvwxyz

RALEWAY

ABCDEFGHIJKLMN
OPQRSTUVWXYZ

SEMIBOLD

abcdefghijklm

HOW TO USE THIS BOOK

She Reads Truth is a community of women dedicated to reading the Word of God every day. In this **John** reading plan, we will read the book of John, along with complementary passages of Scripture, to know more about who Jesus is and how He teaches us to place our faith in Him.

READ & REFLECT

Your **John** book focuses primarily on Scripture, with added features to come alongside your time with God's Word.

SCRIPTURE READING

Designed for a Monday start, this five-week reading plan presents the book of John in daily readings, along with additional passages curated to show how the theme of the main reading can be found throughout Scripture.

Additional passages are marked in your daily reading with the Going Deeper heading.

WORKSHEETS

Each weekday features an interactive worksheet to guide you as you read.

COMMUNITY & CONVERSATION

You can start reading this book at any time! If you want to join women from Upton to the United Kingdom as they read along with you, join us in the **John** reading plan through our app or website and podcast.

 SHE READS TRUTH APP

Devotionals corresponding to each daily reading can be found in the **John** reading plan on the She Reads Truth app. You can use the app to participate in community discussion and more.

GRACE DAY

Use Saturdays to catch up on your reading, pray, and rest in the presence of the Lord.

WEEKLY TRUTH

Sundays are set aside for Scripture memorization.

See tips for memorizing Scripture on page 164.

EXTRAS

This book features additional tools to help you gain a deeper understanding of the text.

Find a complete list of extras on page 15.

 SHEREADSTRUTH.COM

The **John** reading plan and devotionals will also be available at SheReadsTruth.com as the community reads each day. Invite your family, friends, and neighbors to read along with you!

 SHE READS TRUTH PODCAST

Subscribe to the She Reads Truth podcast and join our founders and their guests each week as they talk about the beauty, goodness, and truth they find in Scripture.

 Tune into episodes 298–302 for our **John** series.

The following worksheet will appear at the end of each day's reading. Use it to help you notice some of the unique features and emphases in John's Gospel. Keep in mind, you may not fill out every section each day.

 ————————

During Jesus's time on earth, people from all walks of life were challenged and changed by meeting Him. As you read, take note of how He engaged with specific individuals and groups as well as how each one responded to encountering the Son of God.

 ————————

As one of the disciples in Jesus's inner circle, John drew on his memories of real events when writing this Gospel. Make a note each day of any sensory elements or other specific details you notice.

 ————————

John's Gospel includes statements about both the divinity and humanity of Jesus. Use this space to record statements from the text that help you better understand who Jesus is.

④ ————————

Jesus and others spoke boldly about His purpose and work as the Son of God. Write these statements as you come across them in your reading.

People who interacted with Jesus:	How they responded to Him:	How He engaged with them:
①		

In today's reading there was...

(check all that apply)

○ A miracle

_____

✓ An "I am" statement
   "I am the bread of life."

○ A festival or feast

☒ PASSOVER

☐ FESTIVAL OF TABERNACLES

☐ FESTIVAL OF DEDICATION

☐ OTHER _____

Descriptive details I noticed:

②

Statements about Jesus's identity:	Statements about Jesus's mission:
③	④

TABLE OF

CONTENTS

EXTRAS

In the beginning
was the Word, and
the Word was
with God, and the
Word was God.

SHE READS JOHN

TIME TO READ JOHN
1 hour, 51 minutes

The Gospel of John was most likely written between AD 70 (the date of the destruction of the Second Temple) and AD 100 (the end of John's life). The events in John's Gospel occurred during Jesus's ministry, about AD 30–33.

A LITTLE BACKGROUND

John's original audience was probably composed of people in the larger Greco-Roman world in Ephesus and beyond. His Gospel frequently explains Jewish customs and Palestinian geography and translates Aramaic terms into Greek.

Of all the New Testament books, the Gospel of John most clearly teaches the deity and preexistence of Christ (Jn 1:1–2, 18; 8:58; 17:5, 24; 20:28). John provided proof of Jesus's messiahship by:

1. Narrating seven messianic signs

2. Providing Jesus's seven "I am" statements

3. Including specific instances of fulfilled prophecy, especially at Jesus's death

4. Showing how Jesus fulfilled the symbolism inherent in a variety of Jewish festivals and institutions

MESSAGE & PURPOSE

The purpose statement in 20:30–31 indicates that John wrote his Gospel to reach unbelievers. If the Gospel of John was written after the destruction of the Jewish temple in Jerusalem, it is likely that John sought to present Jesus as the new temple and center of worship for God's people, a replacement of the old sanctuary.

John emphasized the deity of Jesus in the prologue to his Gospel. The prologue affirms that Jesus is the eternal Word (*logos* in the Greek) who was with God and was God. Jesus used the significant phrase "I am" seven times in John, claiming the personal name of God as His own.

GIVE THANKS FOR THE GOSPEL OF JOHN

The Gospel of John is different from the Gospels of Matthew, Mark, and Luke in that over 90 percent of its material is unique. John's Gospel does not focus on the miracles, parables, and public speeches that are so prominent in the other accounts. Instead, John emphasized the identity of Jesus as the Son of God and how we, as believers, should respond to His teachings.

WHO WAS JOHN?

John, the author of the Gospel bearing his name, is also historically known for writing four other books in the New Testament: 1, 2 & 3 John and Revelation. The chart below offers some insight into the life of this New Testament author.

BROTHER

John was the brother of the apostle James. Jesus gave John and James the nickname "Sons of Thunder."

MK 3:17

DISCIPLE OF JOHN THE BAPTIST

Due to John's knowledge of the conversation between Jesus and John the Baptist and his reluctance to refer to himself by name, some scholars believe John was originally a disciple of John the Baptist.

JN 1:29–35

SON

John was a son of Zebedee and Salome.

MT 27:56; MK 3:17; 15:40–41

FISHERMAN

Before he became a disciple of Jesus, John was a fisherman on the Sea of Galilee with his father and brother.

MK 1:16–20

ARROGANT

Early in their ministry, James and John had a haughty streak, asking Jesus for places of honor in glory.

MK 10:37

OBEDIENT

John and Peter were the two disciples sent to secure the upper room and make preparations for the Last Supper.

LK 22:8

CAREGIVER

During the crucifixion, Jesus told John to care for his mother, Mary, and told Mary to care for John.

JN 19:26–27

HUMBLE

Though we see John's arrogance earlier in his ministry, we see him humbly grow throughout the course of his Gospel account. Most likely in a gesture of humility, John usually referred to himself in the third person either as a "disciple" or as "the one Jesus loved."

JN 18:15; 13:23

WELCOMING

John, along with Peter and James, welcomed the newly converted apostle Paul into the community and mission of the Church.

GL 2:9

DISCIPLE OF JESUS

John was one of Jesus's closest disciples, along with Peter and James. The three were the only disciples present for the raising of Jairus's daughter, the transfiguration, and Jesus's anguish in Gethsemane.

MK 14:33; LK 8:51; 9:28; JN 21:24

FEARFUL

John ran when Jesus was arrested, but he summoned the courage to return during Jesus's trial.

MT 26:56; JN 18:15

WITNESS

John was the first of the twelve disciples to recognize the risen Jesus standing on the shore of Galilee after the resurrection.

JN 21:1–7

LEADER

John and Peter were instrumental figures in the establishment of the early Church.

AC 4

PATIENT

John's earlier arrogant posture softened over time. His New Testament writings show that he became an affectionate, patient father in the faith.

1JN 2:28

THE WORD

OF GOD

John 1:1–28

PROLOGUE

[1] In the beginning was the Word, and the Word was with God, and the Word was God. [2] He was with God in the beginning. [3] All things were created through him, and apart from him not one thing was created that has been created. [4] In him was life, and that life was the light of men. [5] That light shines in the darkness, and yet the darkness did not overcome it.

[6] There was a man sent from God whose name was John. [7] He came as a witness to testify about the light, so that all might believe through him. [8] He was not the light, but he came to testify about the light. [9] The true light that gives light to everyone was coming into the world.

[10] He was in the world, and the world was created through him, and yet the world did not recognize him. [11] He came to his own, and his own people did not receive him.

[12] But to all who did receive him, he gave them the right to be children of God, to those who believe in his name,

[13] who were born, not of natural descent, or of the will of the flesh, or of the will of man, but of God.

[14] The Word became flesh and dwelt among us. We observed his glory, the glory as the one and only Son from the Father, full of grace and truth. [15] (John testified concerning him and exclaimed, "This was the one of whom I said, 'The one coming after me ranks ahead of me, because he existed before me.'") [16] Indeed, we have all received grace upon grace from his fullness, [17] for the law was given through Moses; grace and truth came through Jesus Christ. [18] No one has ever seen God. The one and only Son, who is himself God and is at the Father's side—he has revealed him.

JOHN THE BAPTIST'S TESTIMONY

[19] This was John's testimony when the Jews from Jerusalem sent priests and Levites to ask him, "Who are you?"

²⁰ He didn't deny it but confessed, "I am not the Messiah."

²¹ "What then?" they asked him. "Are you Elijah?"

"I am not," he said.

"Are you the Prophet?"

"No," he answered.

²² "Who are you, then?" they asked. "We need to give an answer to those who sent us. What can you tell us about yourself?"

²³ He said, "I am a voice of one crying out in the wilderness: Make straight the way of the Lord—just as Isaiah the prophet said."

²⁴ Now they had been sent from the Pharisees. ²⁵ So they asked him, "Why then do you baptize if you aren't the Messiah, or Elijah, or the Prophet?"

²⁶ "I baptize with water," John answered them. "Someone stands among you, but you don't know him. ²⁷ He is the one coming after me, whose sandal strap I'm not worthy to untie." ²⁸ All this happened in Bethany across the Jordan, where John was baptizing.

◟ GOING DEEPER

Isaiah 55:10–11

¹⁰ "For just as rain and snow fall from heaven
and do not return there
without saturating the earth
and making it germinate and sprout,
and providing seed to sow
and food to eat,
¹¹ so my word that comes from my mouth
will not return to me empty,
but it will accomplish what I please
and will prosper in what I send it to do."

Hebrews 1:1–4

THE NATURE OF THE SON

¹ Long ago God spoke to our ancestors by the prophets at different times and in different ways. ² In these last days, he has spoken to us by his Son. God has appointed him heir of all things and made the universe through him. ³ The Son is the radiance of God's glory and the exact expression of his nature, sustaining all things by his powerful word. After making purification for sins, he sat down at the right hand of the Majesty on high. ⁴ So he became superior to the angels, just as the name he inherited is more excellent than theirs.

People who interacted with Jesus:	How they responded to Him:	How He engaged with them:

In today's reading there was...
(check all that apply)

○ *A miracle*

_____

○ *An "I am" statement*

_____

○ *A festival or feast*

☐ PASSOVER

☐ FESTIVAL OF TABERNACLES

☐ FESTIVAL OF DEDICATION

☐ OTHER _____

Descriptive details I noticed:

Statements about Jesus's identity:	*Statements about Jesus's mission:*

IN THE BIBLE, THE PHRASES "THE WORD OF GOD," "THE WORD OF THE LORD," OR SOMETIMES SIMPLY "THE WORD," ARE USED TO DESCRIBE SEVERAL OF THE DIFFERENT WAYS GOD HAS REVEALED HIMSELF.

In the prologue of John's Gospel, "the Word" is God the Son (Jn 1:1). Rather than using a well-known name for Jesus, John chose to use the Greek word *logos*, meaning "word" or "message," to describe Jesus. In using this Greek term, John communicated specific aspects of Jesus's role and identity. While God's spoken and written words serve as one form of revelation, Jesus as the Word is God's unique revelation of Himself in the flesh. Jesus, the Word, reveals the active power of God in the world. He is the primary means of revelation—the Word that will last forever (RV 22:3–5).

The following Scripture references explore different variations of "word" found in Scripture.

THE

HIS SPOKEN WORD		HIS COMMANDS
EX 3:4–6		EX 20:1–17

SCRIPTURE	HIS JUDGMENT
DT 27:3	HEB 4:12–13

WORD

HIS WORDS SPOKEN BY THE PROPHETS
JR 43:1; HEB 1:1

OF

GOD THE SON		JESUS'S TEACHINGS
JN 1:1–5; HEB 1:2		MK 2:2

THE GOSPEL MESSAGE
AC 13:49

GOD

THE LAMB OF GOD

WEEK 01

John 1:29–51

THE LAMB OF GOD

29 The next day John saw Jesus coming toward him and said, "Look, the Lamb of God, who takes away the sin of the world! 30 This is the one I told you about: 'After me comes a man who ranks ahead of me, because he existed before me.' 31 I didn't know him, but I came baptizing with water so that he might be revealed to Israel." 32 And John testified, "I saw the Spirit descending from heaven like a dove, and he rested on him. 33 I didn't know him, but he who sent me to baptize with water told me, 'The one you see the Spirit descending and resting on—he is the one who baptizes with the Holy Spirit.' 34 I have seen and testified that this is the Son of God."

35 The next day, John was standing with two of his disciples. 36 When he saw Jesus passing by, he said, "Look, the Lamb of God!"

37 The two disciples heard him say this and followed Jesus. 38 When Jesus turned and noticed them following him, he asked them, "What are you looking for?"

They said to him, "Rabbi" (which means "Teacher"), "where are you staying?"

39 "Come and you'll see," he replied. So they went and saw where he was staying, and they stayed with him that day. It was about four in the afternoon.

40 Andrew, Simon Peter's brother, was one of the two who heard John and followed him. 41 He first found his own brother Simon and told him, "We have found the Messiah" (which is translated "the Christ"), 42 and he brought Simon to Jesus.

When Jesus saw him, he said, "You are Simon, son of John. You will be called Cephas" (which is translated "Peter").

43 The next day Jesus decided to leave for Galilee. He found Philip and told him,

"Follow me."

44 Now Philip was from Bethsaida, the hometown of Andrew and Peter. 45 Philip found Nathanael and told him, "We have found the one Moses wrote about in the law (and so did the prophets): Jesus the son of Joseph, from Nazareth."

46 "Can anything good come out of Nazareth?" Nathanael asked him.

"Come and see," Philip answered.

47 Then Jesus saw Nathanael coming toward him and said about him, "Here truly is an Israelite in whom there is no deceit."

48 "How do you know me?" Nathanael asked.

"Before Philip called you, when you were under the fig tree, I saw you," Jesus answered.

49 "Rabbi," Nathanael replied, "You are the Son of God; you are the King of Israel!"

50 Jesus responded to him, "Do you believe because I told you I saw you under the fig tree? You will see greater things than this." 51 Then he said, "Truly I tell you, you will see heaven opened and the angels of God ascending and descending on the Son of Man."

◆ GOING DEEPER

Deuteronomy 18:15–18

15 The LORD your God will raise up for you a prophet like me from among your own brothers. You must listen to him. 16 This is what you requested from the LORD your God at Horeb on the day of the assembly when you said, "Let us not continue to hear the voice of the LORD our God or see this great fire any longer, so that we will not die!" 17 Then the LORD said to me, "They have spoken well. 18 I will raise up for them a prophet like you from among their brothers. I will put my words in his mouth, and he will tell them everything I command him."

Isaiah 53:7–12

7 He was oppressed and afflicted,
yet he did not open his mouth.
Like a lamb led to the slaughter
and like a sheep silent before her shearers,
he did not open his mouth.
8 He was taken away because of oppression and judgment,
and who considered his fate?
For he was cut off from the land of the living;
he was struck because of my people's rebellion.
9 He was assigned a grave with the wicked,
but he was with a rich man at his death,
because he had done no violence
and had not spoken deceitfully.

10 Yet the LORD was pleased to crush him severely.
When you make him a guilt offering,
he will see his seed, he will prolong his days,
and by his hand, the LORD's pleasure will be accomplished.
11 After his anguish,
he will see light and be satisfied.
By his knowledge,
my righteous servant will justify many,
and he will carry their iniquities.
12 Therefore I will give him the many as a portion,
and he will receive the mighty as spoil,
because he willingly submitted to death,
and was counted among the rebels;
yet he bore the sin of many
and interceded for the rebels.

People who interacted with Jesus:	How they responded to Him:	How He engaged with them:

In today's reading there was...

(check all that apply)

○ *A miracle*

_____

○ *An "I am" statement*

_____

○ *A festival or feast*

☐ PASSOVER

☐ FESTIVAL OF TABERNACLES

☐ FESTIVAL OF DEDICATION

☐ OTHER _____

Descriptive details I noticed:

Statements about Jesus's identity:	Statements about Jesus's mission:

WEEK

JESUS DISPLAYS HIS GLORY

01

John 2

THE FIRST SIGN: TURNING WATER INTO WINE

[1] On the third day a wedding took place in Cana of Galilee. Jesus's mother was there, [2] and Jesus and his disciples were invited to the wedding as well. [3] When the wine ran out, Jesus's mother told him, "They don't have any wine."

[4] "What has this concern of yours to do with me, woman?" Jesus asked. "My hour has not yet come."

[5] "Do whatever he tells you," his mother told the servants.

[6] Now six stone water jars had been set there for Jewish purification. Each contained twenty or thirty gallons.

[7] "Fill the jars with water," Jesus told them. So they filled them to the brim. [8] Then he said to them, "Now draw some out and take it to the headwaiter." And they did.

[9] When the headwaiter tasted the water (after it had become wine), he did not know where it came from—though the servants who had drawn the water knew. He called the groom [10] and told him, "Everyone sets out the fine wine first, then, after people are drunk, the inferior. But you have kept the fine wine until now."

[11] Jesus did this, the first of his signs, in Cana of Galilee.

He revealed his glory, and his disciples believed in him.

[12] After this, he went down to Capernaum, together with his mother, his brothers, and his disciples, and they stayed there only a few days.

CLEANSING THE TEMPLE

¹³ The Jewish Passover was near, and so Jesus went up to Jerusalem. ¹⁴ In the temple he found people selling oxen, sheep, and doves, and he also found the money changers sitting there. ¹⁵ After making a whip out of cords, he drove everyone out of the temple with their sheep and oxen. He also poured out the money changers' coins and overturned the tables. ¹⁶ He told those who were selling doves, "Get these things out of here! Stop turning my Father's house into a marketplace!"

¹⁷ And his disciples remembered that it is written: Zeal for your house will consume me.

¹⁸ So the Jews replied to him, "What sign will you show us for doing these things?"

¹⁹ Jesus answered, "Destroy this temple, and I will raise it up in three days."

²⁰ Therefore the Jews said, "This temple took forty-six years to build, and will you raise it up in three days?"

²¹ But he was speaking about the temple of his body. ²² So when he was raised from the dead, his disciples remembered that he had said this, and they believed the Scripture and the statement Jesus had made.

²³ While he was in Jerusalem during the Passover Festival, many believed in his name when they saw the signs he was doing. ²⁴ Jesus, however, would not entrust himself to them, since he knew them all ²⁵ and because he did not need anyone to testify about man; for he himself knew what was in man.

❧ GOING DEEPER

Psalm 104:14–15

¹⁴ He causes grass to grow for the livestock
and provides crops for man to cultivate,
producing food from the earth,
¹⁵ wine that makes human hearts glad—
making his face shine with oil—
and bread that sustains human hearts.

Jeremiah 31:12–14

¹² They will come and shout for joy on the heights of Zion;
they will be radiant with joy
because of the LORD's goodness,
because of the grain, the new wine, the fresh oil,
and because of the young of the flocks and herds.
Their life will be like an irrigated garden,
and they will no longer grow weak from hunger.
¹³ Then the young women will rejoice with dancing,
while young and old men rejoice together.
I will turn their mourning into joy,
give them consolation,
and bring happiness out of grief.

¹⁴ I will refresh the priests
with an abundance,
and my people will be
satisfied with my goodness.

This is the LORD's declaration.

People who interacted with Jesus:	How they responded to Him:	How He engaged with them:

In today's reading there was...
(check all that apply)

○ A miracle

_____

○ An "I am" statement

_____

○ A festival or feast

☐ PASSOVER

☐ FESTIVAL OF TABERNACLES

☐ FESTIVAL OF DEDICATION

☐ OTHER _____

Descriptive details I noticed:

Statements about Jesus's identity:	Statements about Jesus's mission:

THE ONE AND

ONLY SON

John 3

JESUS AND NICODEMUS

¹ There was a man from the Pharisees named Nicodemus, a ruler of the Jews. ² This man came to him at night and said, "Rabbi, we know that you are a teacher who has come from God, for no one could perform these signs you do unless God were with him."

³ Jesus replied, "Truly I tell you, unless someone is born again, he cannot see the kingdom of God."

⁴ "How can anyone be born when he is old?" Nicodemus asked him. "Can he enter his mother's womb a second time and be born?"

⁵ Jesus answered, "Truly I tell you, unless someone is born of water and the Spirit, he cannot enter the kingdom of God. ⁶ Whatever is born of the flesh is flesh, and whatever is born of the Spirit is spirit. ⁷ Do not be amazed that I told you that you must be born again. ⁸ The wind blows where it pleases, and you hear its sound, but you don't know where it comes from or where it is going. So it is with everyone born of the Spirit."

⁹ "How can these things be?" asked Nicodemus.

¹⁰ "Are you a teacher of Israel and don't know these things?" Jesus replied. ¹¹ "Truly I tell you, we speak what we know and we testify to what we have seen, but you do not accept our testimony. ¹² If I have told you about earthly things and you don't believe, how will you believe if I tell you about heavenly things? ¹³ No one has ascended into heaven except the one who descended from heaven—the Son of Man.

¹⁴ "Just as Moses lifted up the snake in the wilderness, so the Son of Man must be lifted up, ¹⁵ so that everyone who believes in him may have eternal life. ¹⁶ For God loved the world in this way: He gave his one and only Son, so that everyone who believes in him will not perish but have eternal life.

¹⁷ For God did not send his Son into the world to condemn the world, but to save the world through him.

¹⁸ Anyone who believes in him is not condemned, but anyone who does not believe is already condemned, because he has not believed in the name of the

one and only Son of God. [19] This is the judgment: The light has come into the world, and people loved darkness rather than the light because their deeds were evil. [20] For everyone who does evil hates the light and avoids it, so that his deeds may not be exposed. [21] But anyone who lives by the truth comes to the light, so that his works may be shown to be accomplished by God."

JESUS AND JOHN THE BAPTIST

[22] After this, Jesus and his disciples went to the Judean countryside, where he spent time with them and baptized.

[23] John also was baptizing in Aenon near Salim, because there was plenty of water there. People were coming and being baptized, [24] since John had not yet been thrown into prison.

[25] Then a dispute arose between John's disciples and a Jew about purification. [26] So they came to John and told him, "Rabbi, the one you testified about, and who was with you across the Jordan, is baptizing—and everyone is going to him."

[27] John responded, "No one can receive anything unless it has been given to him from heaven. [28] You yourselves can testify that I said, 'I am not the Messiah, but I've been sent ahead of him.' [29] He who has the bride is the groom. But the groom's friend, who stands by and listens for him, rejoices greatly at the groom's voice. So this joy of mine is complete. [30] He must increase, but I must decrease."

THE ONE FROM HEAVEN

[31] The one who comes from above is above all. The one who is from the earth is earthly and speaks in earthly terms. The one who comes from heaven is above all. [32] He testifies to what he has seen and heard, and yet no one accepts his testimony. [33] The one who has accepted his testimony has affirmed that God is true. [34] For the one whom God sent speaks God's words, since he gives the Spirit without measure.

[35] The Father loves the Son and has given all things into his hands.

[36] The one who believes in the Son has eternal life, but the one who rejects the Son will not see life; instead, the wrath of God remains on him.

🔖 GOING DEEPER

2 Samuel 7:13

"He is the one who will build a house for my name, and I will establish the throne of his kingdom forever."

Romans 8:31–32

[31] What, then, are we to say about these things? If God is for us, who is against us? [32] He did not even spare his own Son but gave him up for us all. How will he not also with him grant us everything?

1 John 4:9–10

[9] God's love was revealed among us in this way: God sent his one and only Son into the world so that we might live through him. [10] Love consists in this: not that we loved God, but that he loved us and sent his Son to be the atoning sacrifice for our sins.

People who interacted with Jesus:	_How they responded to Him:_	_How He engaged with them:_

In today's reading there was...
(check all that apply)

○ _A miracle_

_____

○ _An "I am" statement_

_____

○ _A festival or feast_

☐ PASSOVER

☐ FESTIVAL OF TABERNACLES

☐ FESTIVAL OF DEDICATION

☐ OTHER _____

Descriptive details I noticed:

Statements about Jesus's identity:	_Statements about Jesus's mission:_

THE LIVING WATER

WEEK 01

JESUS AND THE SAMARITAN WOMAN

¹ When Jesus learned that the Pharisees had heard he was making and baptizing more disciples than John ² (though Jesus himself was not baptizing, but his disciples were), ³ he left Judea and went again to Galilee. ⁴ He had to travel through Samaria; ⁵ so he came to a town of Samaria called Sychar near the property that Jacob had given his son Joseph. ⁶ Jacob's well was there, and Jesus, worn out from his journey, sat down at the well. It was about noon.

⁷ A woman of Samaria came to draw water.

"Give me a drink," Jesus said to her, ⁸ because his disciples had gone into town to buy food.

⁹ "How is it that you, a Jew, ask for a drink from me, a Samaritan woman?" she asked him. For Jews do not associate with Samaritans.

¹⁰ Jesus answered, "If you knew the gift of God, and who is saying to you, 'Give me a drink,' you would ask him, and he would give you living water."

¹¹ "Sir," said the woman, "you don't even have a bucket, and the well is deep. So where do you get this 'living water'? ¹² You aren't greater than our father Jacob, are you? He gave us the well and drank from it himself, as did his sons and livestock."

¹³ Jesus said, "Everyone who drinks from this water will get thirsty again. ¹⁴ But whoever drinks from the water that I will give him will never get thirsty again. In fact, the water I will give him will become a well of water springing up in him for eternal life."

¹⁵ "Sir," the woman said to him, "give me this water so that I won't get thirsty and come here to draw water."

¹⁶ "Go call your husband," he told her, "and come back here."

¹⁷ "I don't have a husband," she answered.

"You have correctly said, 'I don't have a husband,'" Jesus said. ¹⁸ "For you've had five husbands, and the man you now have is not your husband. What you have said is true."

¹⁹ "Sir," the woman replied, "I see that you are a prophet. ²⁰ Our ancestors worshiped on this mountain, but you Jews say that the place to worship is in Jerusalem."

²¹ Jesus told her, "Believe me, woman, an hour is coming when you will worship the Father neither on this mountain nor in Jerusalem. ²² You Samaritans worship what you do not know. We worship what we do know, because salvation is from the Jews.

²³ But an hour is coming, and is now here, when the true worshipers will worship the Father in Spirit and in truth. Yes, the Father wants such people to worship him.

²⁴ God is spirit, and those who worship him must worship in Spirit and in truth."

²⁵ The woman said to him, "I know that the Messiah is coming" (who is called Christ). "When he comes, he will explain everything to us."

²⁶ Jesus told her, "I, the one speaking to you, am he."

THE RIPENED HARVEST

²⁷ Just then his disciples arrived, and they were amazed that he was talking with a woman. Yet no one said, "What do you want?" or "Why are you talking with her?"

²⁸ Then the woman left her water jar, went into town, and told the people, ²⁹ "Come, see a man who told me everything I ever did. Could this be the Messiah?" ³⁰ They left the town and made their way to him.

31 In the meantime the disciples kept urging him, "Rabbi, eat something."

32 But he said, "I have food to eat that you don't know about."

33 The disciples said to one another, "Could someone have brought him something to eat?"

34 "My food is to do the will of him who sent me and to finish his work," Jesus told them. 35 "Don't you say, 'There are still four more months, and then comes the harvest'? Listen to what I'm telling you: Open your eyes and look at the fields, because they are ready for harvest. 36 The reaper is already receiving pay and gathering fruit for eternal life, so that the sower and reaper can rejoice together. 37 For in this case the saying is true: 'One sows and another reaps.' 38 I sent you to reap what you didn't labor for; others have labored, and you have benefited from their labor."

THE SAVIOR OF THE WORLD

39 Now many Samaritans from that town believed in him because of what the woman said when she testified, "He told me everything I ever did." 40 So when the Samaritans came to him, they asked him to stay with them, and he stayed there two days. 41 Many more believed because of what he said. 42 And they told the woman, "We no longer believe because of what you said, since we have heard for ourselves and know that this really is the Savior of the world."

A GALILEAN WELCOME

43 After two days he left there for Galilee. 44 (Jesus himself had testified that a prophet has no honor in his own country.) 45 When they entered Galilee, the Galileans welcomed him because they had seen everything he did in Jerusalem during the festival. For they also had gone to the festival.

THE SECOND SIGN: HEALING AN OFFICIAL'S SON

46 He went again to Cana of Galilee, where he had turned the water into wine. There was a certain royal official whose son was ill at Capernaum. 47 When this man heard that Jesus had come from Judea into Galilee, he went to him and pleaded with him to come down and heal his son, since he was about to die.

48 Jesus told him, "Unless you people see signs and wonders, you will not believe."

49 "Sir," the official said to him, "come down before my boy dies."

[50] "Go," Jesus told him, "your son will live." The man believed what Jesus said to him and departed.

[51] While he was still going down, his servants met him saying that his boy was alive. [52] He asked them at what time he got better. "Yesterday at one in the afternoon the fever left him," they answered. [53] The father realized this was the very hour at which Jesus had told him, "Your son will live." So he himself believed, along with his whole household.

[54] Now this was also the second sign Jesus performed after he came from Judea to Galilee.

🛡 GOING DEEPER

Isaiah 55:1–3

COME TO THE LORD

[1] "Come, everyone who is thirsty,
come to the water;
and you without silver,
come, buy, and eat!
Come, buy wine and milk
without silver and without cost!
[2] Why do you spend silver on what is not food,
and your wages on what does not satisfy?
Listen carefully to me, and eat what is good,
and you will enjoy the choicest of foods.
[3] Pay attention and come to me;
listen, so that you will live.
I will make a permanent covenant with you
on the basis of the faithful kindnesses of David."

People who interacted with Jesus:	How they responded to Him:	How He engaged with them:

In today's reading there was...
(check all that apply)

○ *A miracle*

_____

○ *An "I am" statement*

_____

○ *A festival or feast*

☐ PASSOVER

☐ FESTIVAL OF TABERNACLES

☐ FESTIVAL OF DEDICATION

☐ OTHER _____

Descriptive details I noticed:

Statements about Jesus's identity:	Statements about Jesus's mission:

GRACE

DAY

Take this day
to catch up on
your reading,
pray, and rest in
the presence
of the Lord.

The Son is the
radiance of God's
glory and the exact
expression of his
nature, sustaining
all things by his
powerful word.

HEBREWS 1:3

WEEKLY

Scripture is God breathed and true. When we memorize it, we carry the good news of Jesus with us wherever we go.

During this study, we will memorize the first five verses from John's Gospel. In his prologue, John used poetic language to describe the identity and nature of Jesus. This week we will memorize the first verse of this passage, which identifies Jesus—the Word—as God Himself.

TRUTH

In the beginning was the Word, and the Word was with God, and the Word was God. He was with God in the beginning. All things were created through him, and apart from him not one thing was created that has been created. In him was life, and that life was the light of men. That light shines in the darkness, and yet the darkness did not overcome it.

JOHN 1:1–5

See tips for memorizing Scripture on page 164.

HEALING ON THE SABBATH

WEEK 02

JESUS RESPONDED TO THEM. "MY FATHER IS STILL WORKING, AND I AM WORKING ALSO." —JOHN 5:17

John 5:1–30

THE THIRD SIGN: HEALING THE SICK

¹ After this, a Jewish festival took place, and Jesus went up to Jerusalem. ² By the Sheep Gate in Jerusalem there is a pool, called Bethesda in Aramaic, which has five colonnades. ³ Within these lay a large number of the disabled—blind, lame, and paralyzed.

⁵ One man was there who had been disabled for thirty-eight years. ⁶ When Jesus saw him lying there and realized he had already been there a long time, he said to him,

"Do you want to get well?"

⁷ "Sir," the disabled man answered, "I have no one to put me into the pool when the water is stirred up, but while I'm coming, someone goes down ahead of me."

⁸ "Get up," Jesus told him, "pick up your mat and walk." ⁹ Instantly the man got well, picked up his mat, and started to walk.

Now that day was the Sabbath, ¹⁰ and so the Jews said to the man who had been healed, "This is the Sabbath. The law prohibits you from picking up your mat."

¹¹ He replied, "The man who made me well told me, 'Pick up your mat and walk.'"

¹² "Who is this man who told you, 'Pick up your mat and walk'?" they asked. ¹³ But the man who was healed did not know who it was, because Jesus had slipped away into the crowd that was there.

¹⁴ After this, Jesus found him in the temple and said to him, "See, you are well. Do not sin anymore, so that something worse doesn't happen to you." ¹⁵ The man went and reported to the Jews that it was Jesus who had made him well. ¹⁶ Therefore, the Jews began persecuting Jesus because he was doing these things on the Sabbath.

HONORING THE FATHER AND THE SON

[17] Jesus responded to them, "My Father is still working, and I am working also." [18] This is why the Jews began trying all the more to kill him: Not only was he breaking the Sabbath, but he was even calling God his own Father, making himself equal to God.

[19] Jesus replied, "Truly I tell you, the Son is not able to do anything on his own, but only what he sees the Father doing. For whatever the Father does, the Son likewise does these things. [20] For the Father loves the Son and shows him everything he is doing, and he will show him greater works than these so that you will be amazed. [21] And just as the Father raises the dead and gives them life, so the Son also gives life to whom he wants. [22] The Father, in fact, judges no one but has given all judgment to the Son, [23] so that all people may honor the Son just as they honor the Father. Anyone who does not honor the Son does not honor the Father who sent him.

LIFE AND JUDGMENT

[24] "Truly I tell you, anyone who hears my word and believes him who sent me has eternal life and will not come under judgment but has passed from death to life.

[25] "Truly I tell you, an hour is coming, and is now here, when the dead will hear the voice of the Son of God, and those who hear will live. [26] For just as the Father has life in himself, so also he has granted to the Son to have life in himself. [27] And he has granted him the right to pass judgment, because he is the Son of Man. [28] Do not be amazed at this, because a time is coming when all who are in the graves will hear his voice [29] and come out—those who have done good things, to the resurrection of life, but those who have done wicked things, to the resurrection of condemnation.

[30] "I can do nothing on my own. I judge only as I hear, and my judgment is just, because

I do not seek my own will, but the will of him who sent me."

GOING DEEPER

Exodus 20:8–11

[8] "Remember the Sabbath day, to keep it holy: [9] You are to labor six days and do all your work, [10] but the seventh day is a Sabbath to the LORD your God. You must not do any work—you, your son or daughter, your male or female servant, your livestock, or the resident alien who is within your city gates. [11] For the LORD made the heavens and the earth, the sea, and everything in them in six days; then he rested on the seventh day. Therefore the LORD blessed the Sabbath day and declared it holy."

Luke 6:1–11

LORD OF THE SABBATH

[1] On a Sabbath, he passed through the grainfields. His disciples were picking heads of grain, rubbing them in their hands, and eating them. [2] But some of the Pharisees said, "Why are you doing what is not lawful on the Sabbath?"

[3] Jesus answered them, "Haven't you read what David and those who were with him did when he was hungry— [4] how he entered the house of God and took and ate the bread of the Presence, which is not lawful for any but the priests to eat? He even gave some to those who were with him." [5] Then he told them, "The Son of Man is Lord of the Sabbath."

[6] On another Sabbath he entered the synagogue and was teaching. A man was there whose right hand was shriveled. [7] The scribes and Pharisees were watching him closely, to see if he would heal on the Sabbath, so that they could find a charge against him. [8] But he knew their thoughts and told the man with the shriveled hand, "Get up and stand here." So he got up and stood there. [9] Then Jesus said to them, "I ask you: Is it lawful to do good on the Sabbath or to do evil, to save life or to destroy it?" [10] After looking around at them all, he told him, "Stretch out your hand." He did, and his hand was restored. [11] They, however, were filled with rage and started discussing with one another what they might do to Jesus.

People who interacted with Jesus:	How they responded to Him:	How He engaged with them:

In today's reading there was...

(check all that apply)

○ A miracle

_____

○ An "I am" statement

_____

○ A festival or feast

☐ PASSOVER

☐ FESTIVAL OF TABERNACLES

☐ FESTIVAL OF DEDICATION

☐ OTHER _____

Descriptive details I noticed:

Statements about Jesus's identity:	Statements about Jesus's mission:

JESUS FEEDS THE FIVE THOUSAND

—

John 5:31–47

WITNESSES TO JESUS

³¹ "If I testify about myself, my testimony is not true. ³² There is another who testifies about me, and I know that the testimony he gives about me is true. ³³ You sent messengers to John, and he testified to the truth. ³⁴ I don't receive human testimony, but I say these things so that you may be saved. ³⁵ John was a burning and shining lamp, and you were willing to rejoice for a while in his light.

³⁶ "But I have a greater testimony than John's because of the works that the Father has given me to accomplish. These very works I am doing testify about me that the Father has sent me. ³⁷ The Father who sent me has himself testified about me. You have not heard his voice at any time, and you haven't seen his form. ³⁸ You don't have his word residing in you, because you don't believe the one he sent. ³⁹ You pore over the Scriptures because you think you have eternal life in them, and yet they testify about me. ⁴⁰ But you are not willing to come to me so that you may have life.

⁴¹ "I do not accept glory from people, ⁴² but I know you—that you have no love for God within you. ⁴³ I have come in my Father's name, and yet you don't accept me. If someone else comes in his own name, you will accept him. ⁴⁴ How can you believe, since you accept glory from one another but don't seek the glory that comes from the only God? ⁴⁵ Do not think that I will accuse you to the Father. Your accuser is Moses, on whom you have set your hope. ⁴⁶ For if you believed Moses, you would believe me, because he wrote about me. ⁴⁷ But if you don't believe what he wrote, how will you believe my words?"

John 6:1–21

THE FOURTH SIGN: FEEDING OF THE FIVE THOUSAND

¹ After this, Jesus crossed the Sea of Galilee (or Tiberias). ² A huge crowd was following him because they saw the signs that he was performing by healing the sick. ³ Jesus went up a mountain and sat down there with his disciples.

⁴ Now the Passover, a Jewish festival, was near. ⁵ So when Jesus looked up and noticed a huge crowd coming toward him, he asked Philip, "Where will we buy bread so that these people can eat?" ⁶ He asked this to test him, for he himself knew what he was going to do.

⁷ Philip answered him, "Two hundred denarii worth of bread wouldn't be enough for each of them to have a little."

8 One of his disciples, Andrew, Simon Peter's brother, said to him, 9 "There's a boy here who has five barley loaves and two fish—but what are they for so many?"

10 Jesus said, "Have the people sit down."

There was plenty of grass in that place; so they sat down. The men numbered about five thousand. 11 Then Jesus took the loaves, and after giving thanks he distributed them to those who were seated—so also with the fish, as much as they wanted.

12 When they were full, he told his disciples, "Collect the leftovers so that nothing is wasted." 13 So they collected them and filled twelve baskets with the pieces from the five barley loaves that were left over by those who had eaten.

14 When the people saw the sign he had done, they said,

"This truly is the Prophet who is to come into the world."

15 Therefore, when Jesus realized that they were about to come and take him by force to make him king, he withdrew again to the mountain by himself.

THE FIFTH SIGN: WALKING ON WATER

16 When evening came, his disciples went down to the sea, 17 got into a boat, and started across the sea to Capernaum. Darkness had already set in, but Jesus had not yet come to them. 18 A high wind arose, and the sea began to churn. 19 After they had rowed about three or four miles, they saw Jesus walking on the sea. He was coming near the boat, and they were afraid. 20 But he said to them, "It is I. Don't be afraid." 21 Then they were willing to take him on board, and at once the boat was at the shore where they were heading.

🛡 GOING DEEPER

Numbers 11:21–23

21 But Moses replied, "I'm in the middle of a people with six hundred thousand foot soldiers, yet you say, 'I will give them meat, and they will eat for a month.' 22 If flocks and herds were slaughtered for them, would they have enough? Or if all the fish in the sea were caught for them, would they have enough?"

23 The LORD answered Moses, "Is the LORD's arm weak? Now you will see whether or not what I have promised will happen to you."

2 Kings 4:42–44

THE MULTIPLIED BREAD

42 A man from Baal-shalishah came to the man of God with his sack full of twenty loaves of barley bread from the first bread of the harvest. Elisha said, "Give it to the people to eat."

43 But Elisha's attendant asked, "What? Am I to set this before a hundred men?"

"Give it to the people to eat," Elisha said, "for this is what the LORD says: 'They will eat, and they will have some left over.'" 44 So he set it before them, and as the LORD had promised, they ate and had some left over.

People who interacted with Jesus:	How they responded to Him:	How He engaged with them:

In today's reading there was...

(check all that apply)

○ A miracle

_____

○ An "I am" statement

_____

○ A festival or feast

☐ PASSOVER

☐ FESTIVAL OF TABERNACLES

☐ FESTIVAL OF DEDICATION

☐ OTHER _____

Descriptive details I noticed:

Statements about Jesus's identity:	Statements about Jesus's mission:

THE BREAD OF LIFE

John 6:22–71

THE BREAD OF LIFE

22 The next day, the crowd that had stayed on the other side of the sea saw there had been only one boat. They also saw that Jesus had not boarded the boat with his disciples, but that his disciples had gone off alone. 23 Some boats from Tiberias came near the place where they had eaten the bread after the Lord had given thanks. 24 When the crowd saw that neither Jesus nor his disciples were there, they got into the boats and went to Capernaum looking for Jesus. 25 When they found him on the other side of the sea, they said to him, "Rabbi, when did you get here?"

26 Jesus answered, "Truly I tell you, you are looking for me, not because you saw the signs, but because you ate the loaves and were filled. 27 Don't work for the food that perishes but for the food that lasts for eternal life, which the Son of Man will give you, because God the Father has set his seal of approval on him."

28 "What can we do to perform the works of God?" they asked.

29 Jesus replied, "This is the work of God—that you believe in the one he has sent."

30 "What sign, then, are you going to do so that we may see and believe you?" they asked. "What are you going to perform? 31 Our ancestors ate the manna in the wilderness, just as it is written: He gave them bread from heaven to eat."

32 Jesus said to them, "Truly I tell you, Moses didn't give you the bread from heaven, but my Father gives you the true bread from heaven. 33 For the bread of God is the one who comes down from heaven and gives life to the world."

34 Then they said, "Sir, give us this bread always."

35 "I am the bread of life," Jesus told them. "No one who comes to me will ever be hungry, and no one who believes in me will ever be thirsty again. 36 But as I told you, you've seen me, and yet you do not believe. 37 Everyone the Father gives me will come to me, and the one who comes to me I will never cast out. 38 For I have come down from heaven, not to do my own will, but the will of him who sent me. 39 This is the will of him who sent me: that I should lose none of those he has given me but should raise them up on the last day. 40 For this is the will of my Father: that everyone who sees the Son and believes in him will have eternal life, and I will raise him up on the last day."

41 Therefore the Jews started grumbling about him because he said, "I am the bread that came down from heaven." 42 They were saying, "Isn't this Jesus the son of Joseph, whose father and mother we know? How can he now say, 'I have come down from heaven'?"

43 Jesus answered them, "Stop grumbling among yourselves. 44 No one can come to me unless the Father who sent me draws him, and I will raise him up on the last day. 45 It is written in the Prophets: And they will all be taught by God. Everyone who has listened to and learned from the Father comes to me— 46 not that anyone has seen the Father except the one who is from God. He has seen the Father.

47 "Truly I tell you, anyone who believes has eternal life. 48 I am the bread of life. 49 Your ancestors ate the manna in the wilderness, and they died. 50 This is the bread that comes down from heaven so that anyone may eat of it and not die. 51 I am the living bread that came down from heaven. If anyone eats of this bread he will live forever. The bread that I will give for the life of the world is my flesh."

52 At that, the Jews argued among themselves, "How can this man give us his flesh to eat?"

53 So Jesus said to them, "Truly I tell you, unless you eat the flesh of the Son of Man and drink his blood, you do not have life in yourselves. 54 The one who eats my flesh and drinks my blood has eternal life, and I will raise him up on the last day, 55 because my flesh is true food and my blood is true drink. 56 The one who eats my flesh and drinks my blood remains in me, and I in him. 57 Just as the living Father sent me and I live because of the Father, so the one who feeds on me will live because of me. 58 This is the bread that came down from heaven; it is not like the manna your ancestors ate—and they died. The one who eats this bread will live forever."

59 He said these things while teaching in the synagogue in Capernaum.

MANY DISCIPLES DESERT JESUS

60 Therefore, when many of his disciples heard this, they said, "This teaching is hard. Who can accept it?"

61 Jesus, knowing in himself that his disciples were grumbling about this, asked them, "Does this offend you? 62 Then what if you were to observe the Son of Man ascending to where he was before? 63 The Spirit is the one who gives life. The flesh doesn't help at all. The words that I have spoken to you are spirit and are life. 64 But there are some among you who don't believe." (For Jesus knew from

the beginning those who did not believe and the one who would betray him.) [65] He said, "This is why I told you that no one can come to me unless it is granted to him by the Father."

[66] From that moment many of his disciples turned back and no longer accompanied him. [67] So Jesus said to the Twelve, "You don't want to go away too, do you?"

[68] Simon Peter answered,

"Lord, to whom will we go? You have the words of eternal life.

[69] We have come to believe and know that you are the Holy One of God."

[70] Jesus replied to them, "Didn't I choose you, the Twelve? Yet one of you is a devil." [71] He was referring to Judas, Simon Iscariot's son, one of the Twelve, because he was going to betray him.

🛡 GOING DEEPER

Exodus 16:4–5

[4] Then the LORD said to Moses, "I am going to rain bread from heaven for you. The people are to go out each day and gather enough for that day. This way I will test them to see whether or not they will follow my instructions. [5] On the sixth day, when they prepare what they bring in, it will be twice as much as they gather on other days."

Jeremiah 31:25

"For I satisfy the thirsty person and feed all those who are weak."

People who interacted with Jesus:	How they responded to Him:	How He engaged with them:

In today's reading there was...

(check all that apply)

○ A miracle

_____

○ An "I am" statement

_____

○ A festival or feast

☐ PASSOVER

☐ FESTIVAL OF TABERNACLES

☐ FESTIVAL OF DEDICATION

☐ OTHER _____

Descriptive details I noticed:

Statements about Jesus's identity:	Statements about Jesus's mission:

JESUS'S "I AM"

"I am," or *ego eimi* in New Testament Greek, is a simple phrase with rich meaning. In the Septuagint, the ancient Greek translation of the Old Testament, this phrase was part of the divine name God revealed to Moses from the burning bush in Exodus 3:14.

God replied to Moses, "I AM *[ego eimi]* WHO I AM. This is what you are to say to the Israelites: 'I AM has sent me to you.'"

In the Gospel of John, Jesus used *ego eimi* with seven metaphors to reveal key truths about His deity and character.

On the page that follows, we've included a list of Jesus's "I am" statements in the Gospel of John, with the *ego eimi* marked in bold, along with cross-references that highlight their connections to the Old Testament and other relevant passages in John.

STATEMENTS

JN 6:35

See also: Ex 16; Dt 8:3;
Ps 78:23–25; Jn 6:48

"**I am** the bread of life," Jesus told them. "No one who comes to me will ever be hungry, and no one who believes in me will ever be thirsty again."

JN 8:12

See also: Ex 13:17–22;
Is 9:2; 42:6; 49:6; Jn 9:5

Jesus spoke to them again: "**I am** the light of the world. Anyone who follows me will never walk in the darkness but will have the light of life."

JN 10:7

See also: Nm 27:15–17;
Ps 118:19–20; 121:8; Jn 10:9

Jesus said again, "Truly I tell you, **I am** the gate for the sheep."

JN 10:11

See also: Ps 23;
Ezk 34:10–16; Mc 5:4; Jn 10:14

"**I am** the good shepherd. The good shepherd lays down his life for the sheep."

JN 11:25

See also: Gn 1–3;
Jb 19:25–27; Is 26:19; 53:10

Jesus said to her, "**I am** the resurrection and the life. The one who believes in me, even if he dies, will live."

JN 14:6

See also: Gn 12:3; Dt 18:15;
Ps 40:6–9; Is 28:16; 61:1–3

Jesus told him, "**I am** the way, the truth, and the life. No one comes to the Father except through me."

JN 15:1

See also: Ps 80:7–19;
Is 11:10; 27:2–6; Zch 3:8; Jn 15:5

"**I am** the true vine, and my Father is the gardener."

THE UNLIKELY MESSIAH

WEEK 02

John 7:1–52

THE UNBELIEF OF JESUS'S BROTHERS

[1] After this, Jesus traveled in Galilee, since he did not want to travel in Judea because the Jews were trying to kill him. [2] The Jewish Festival of Shelters was near. [3] So his brothers said to him, "Leave here and go to Judea so that your disciples can see your works that you are doing. [4] For no one does anything in secret while he's seeking public recognition. If you do these things, show yourself to the world." [5] (For not even his brothers believed in him.)

[6] Jesus told them, "My time has not yet arrived, but your time is always at hand. [7] The world cannot hate you, but it does hate me because I testify about it—that its works are evil. [8] Go up to the festival yourselves. I'm not going up to this festival, because my time has not yet fully come." [9] After he had said these things, he stayed in Galilee.

JESUS AT THE FESTIVAL OF SHELTERS

[10] After his brothers had gone up to the festival, then he also went up, not openly but secretly. [11] The Jews were looking for him at the festival and saying, "Where is he?" [12] And there was a lot of murmuring about him among the crowds. Some were saying, "He's a good man." Others were saying, "No, on the contrary, he's deceiving the people." [13] Still, nobody was talking publicly about him for fear of the Jews.

[14] When the festival was already half over, Jesus went up into the temple and began to teach. [15] Then the Jews were amazed and said, "How is this man so learned, since he hasn't been trained?"

[16] Jesus answered them, "My teaching isn't mine but is from the one who sent me. [17] If anyone wants to do his will, he will know whether the teaching is from God or whether I am speaking on my own. [18] The one who speaks on his own seeks his own glory; but he who seeks the glory of the one who sent him is true, and there is no unrighteousness in him. [19] Didn't Moses give you the law? Yet none of you keeps the law. Why are you trying to kill me?"

[20] "You have a demon!" the crowd responded. "Who is trying to kill you?"

[21] "I performed one work, and you are all amazed," Jesus answered. [22] "This is why Moses has given you circumcision—not that it comes from Moses but from the fathers—and you circumcise a man on the Sabbath. [23] If a man receives circumcision on the Sabbath so that the law of Moses won't be broken, are you angry at me because I made a man entirely well on the Sabbath? [24] Stop judging according to outward appearances; rather judge according to righteous judgment."

THE IDENTITY OF THE MESSIAH

[25] Some of the people of Jerusalem were saying, "Isn't this the man they are trying to kill? [26] Yet, look, he's speaking publicly and they're saying nothing to him. Can it be true that the authorities know he is the Messiah? [27] But we know where this man is from. When the Messiah comes, nobody will know where he is from."

[28] As he was teaching in the temple, Jesus cried out, "You know me and you know where I am from. Yet I have not come on my own, but the one who sent me is true. You don't know him; [29] I know him because I am from him, and he sent me."

[30] Then they tried to seize him. Yet no one laid a hand on him because his hour had not yet come. [31] However, many from the crowd believed in him and said, "When the Messiah comes, he won't perform more signs than this man has done, will he?" [32] The Pharisees heard the crowd murmuring these things about him, and so the chief priests and the Pharisees sent servants to arrest him.

[33] Then Jesus said, "I am only with you for a short time. Then I'm going to the one who sent me. [34] You will look for me, but you will not find me; and where I am, you cannot come."

³⁵ Then the Jews said to one another, "Where does he intend to go that we won't find him? He doesn't intend to go to the Jewish people dispersed among the Greeks and teach the Greeks, does he? ³⁶ What is this remark he made: 'You will look for me, and you will not find me; and where I am, you cannot come'?"

THE PROMISE OF THE SPIRIT

³⁷ On the last and most important day of the festival, Jesus stood up and cried out, "If anyone is thirsty, let him come to me and drink.

³⁸ The one who believes in me, as the Scripture has said, will have streams of living water flow from deep within him."

³⁹ He said this about the Spirit. Those who believed in Jesus were going to receive the Spirit, for the Spirit had not yet been given because Jesus had not yet been glorified.

THE PEOPLE ARE DIVIDED OVER JESUS

⁴⁰ When some from the crowd heard these words, they said, "This truly is the Prophet." ⁴¹ Others said, "This is the Messiah." But some said, "Surely the Messiah doesn't come from Galilee, does he? ⁴² Doesn't the Scripture say that the Messiah comes from David's offspring and from the town of Bethlehem, where David lived?" ⁴³ So the crowd was divided because of him. ⁴⁴ Some of them wanted to seize him, but no one laid hands on him.

DEBATE OVER JESUS'S CLAIMS

⁴⁵ Then the servants came to the chief priests and Pharisees, who asked them, "Why didn't you bring him?"

⁴⁶ The servants answered, "No man ever spoke like this!"

⁴⁷ Then the Pharisees responded to them, "Are you fooled too? ⁴⁸ Have any of the rulers or Pharisees believed in him? ⁴⁹ But this crowd, which doesn't know the law, is accursed."

⁵⁰ Nicodemus—the one who came to him previously and who was one of them—said to them, ⁵¹ "Our law doesn't judge a man before it hears from him and knows what he's doing, does it?"

⁵² "You aren't from Galilee too, are you?" they replied. "Investigate and you will see that no prophet arises from Galilee."

Isaiah 9:1

Nevertheless, the gloom of the distressed land will not be like that of the former times when he humbled the land of Zebulun and the land of Naphtali. But in the future he will bring honor to the way of the sea, to the land east of the Jordan, and to Galilee of the nations.

Matthew 7:28–29

[28] When Jesus had finished saying these things, the crowds were astonished at his teaching, [29] because he was teaching them like one who had authority, and not like their scribes.

Luke 4:20–24

[20] He then rolled up the scroll, gave it back to the attendant, and sat down. And the eyes of everyone in the synagogue were fixed on him. [21] He began by saying to them, "Today as you listen, this Scripture has been fulfilled."

[22] They were all speaking well of him and were amazed by the gracious words that came from his mouth; yet they said, "Isn't this Joseph's son?"

[23] Then he said to them, "No doubt you will quote this proverb to me: 'Doctor, heal yourself. What we've heard that took place in Capernaum, do here in your hometown also.'"

[24] He also said, "Truly I tell you, no prophet is accepted in his hometown."

People who interacted with Jesus:	How they responded to Him:	How He engaged with them:

In today's reading there was...

(check all that apply)

    ○ A miracle

    _____

    ○ An "I am" statement

    _____

    ○ A festival or feast

        ☐ PASSOVER

        ☐ FESTIVAL OF TABERNACLES

        ☐ FESTIVAL OF DEDICATION

        ☐ OTHER _____

Descriptive details I noticed:

Statements about Jesus's identity:	Statements about Jesus's mission:

THE LIGHT OF

DAY 12

WEEK 02

THE WORLD

John 7:53

*[Then each one went to his house.

John 8:1–30

¹ But Jesus went to the Mount of Olives.

AN ADULTERESS FORGIVEN

² At dawn he went to the temple again, and all the people were coming to him. He sat down and began to teach them.

³ Then the scribes and the Pharisees brought a woman caught in adultery, making her stand in the center. ⁴ "Teacher," they said to him, "this woman was caught in the act of committing adultery. ⁵ In the law Moses commanded us to stone such women. So what do you say?" ⁶ They asked this to trap him, in order that they might have evidence to accuse him.

Jesus stooped down and started writing on the ground with his finger. ⁷ When they persisted in questioning him, he stood up and said to them, "The one without sin among you should be the first to throw a stone at her." ⁸ Then he stooped down again and continued writing on the ground. ⁹ When they heard this, they left one by one, starting with the older men. Only he was left, with the woman in the center. ¹⁰ When Jesus stood up, he said to her, "Woman, where are they? Has no one condemned you?"

¹¹ "No one, Lord," she answered.

"Neither do I condemn you," said Jesus. "Go, and from now on do not sin anymore."]

THE LIGHT OF THE WORLD

¹² Jesus spoke to them again: "I am the light of the world.

Anyone who follows me will never walk in the darkness but will have the light of life."

¹³ So the Pharisees said to him, "You are testifying about yourself. Your testimony is not valid."

¹⁴ "Even if I testify about myself," Jesus replied, "My testimony is true, because I know where I came from and where I'm going. But you don't know where I come from or where I'm going. ¹⁵ You judge by human standards. I judge no one. ¹⁶ And if I do judge, my judgment is true, because it is not I alone who judge, but I and the Father who sent me. ¹⁷ Even in your law it is written that the testimony of two witnesses is true. ¹⁸ I am the one who testifies about myself, and the Father who sent me testifies about me."

¹⁹ Then they asked him, "Where is your Father?"

"You know neither me nor my Father," Jesus answered. "If you knew me, you would also know my Father." ²⁰ He spoke these words by the treasury, while teaching in the temple. But no one seized him, because his hour had not yet come.

JESUS PREDICTS HIS DEPARTURE

²¹ Then he said to them again, "I'm going away; you will look for me, and you will die in your sin. Where I'm going, you cannot come."

²² So the Jews said again, "He won't kill himself, will he, since he says, 'Where I'm going, you cannot come'?"

²³ "You are from below," he told them, "I am from above. You are of this world; I am not of this world. ²⁴ Therefore I told you that you will die in your sins. For if you do not believe that I am he, you will die in your sins."

²⁵ "Who are you?" they questioned.

"Exactly what I've been telling you from the very beginning," Jesus told them. ²⁶ "I have many things to say and to judge about you, but the one who sent me is true, and what I have heard from him—these things I tell the world."

---

*The earliest manuscripts do not include 7:53–8:11.

27 They did not know he was speaking to them about the Father. 28 So Jesus said to them, "When you lift up the Son of Man, then you will know that I am he, and that I do nothing on my own. But just as the Father taught me, I say these things. 29 The one who sent me is with me. He has not left me alone, because I always do what pleases him."

TRUTH AND FREEDOM

30 As he was saying these things, many believed in him.

🛡 GOING DEEPER

Isaiah 60:19–22

19 The sun will no longer be your light by day,
and the brightness of the moon will not shine on you.

> ## The LORD will be your
> ## everlasting light,
> ## and your God will be
> ## your splendor.

20 Your sun will no longer set,
and your moon will not fade;
for the LORD will be your everlasting light,
and the days of your sorrow will be over.
21 All your people will be righteous;
they will possess the land forever;
they are the branch I planted,
the work of my hands,
so that I may be glorified.
22 The least will become a thousand,
the smallest a mighty nation.
I am the LORD;
I will accomplish it quickly in its time.

1 John 1:5–7
FELLOWSHIP WITH GOD

5 This is the message we have heard from him and declare to you: God is light, and there is absolutely no darkness in him. 6 If we say, "We have fellowship with him," and yet we walk in darkness, we are lying and are not practicing the truth. 7 If we walk in the light as he himself is in the light, we have fellowship with one another, and the blood of Jesus his Son cleanses us from all sin.

1 John 2:8

Yet I am writing you a new command, which is true in him and in you, because the darkness is passing away and the true light is already shining.

People who interacted with Jesus:	How they responded to Him:	How He engaged with them:

In today's reading there was...
(check all that apply)

O *A miracle*

_____

O *An "I am" statement*

_____

O *A festival or feast*

☐ PASSOVER

☐ FESTIVAL OF TABERNACLES

☐ FESTIVAL OF DEDICATION

☐ OTHER _____

Descriptive details I noticed:

Statements about Jesus's identity:	Statements about Jesus's mission:

GRACE

DAY

Take this day
to catch up on
your reading,
pray, and rest in
the presence
of the Lord.

"For I satisfy the
thirsty person
and feed all those
who are weak."

JEREMIAH 31:25 ——————————————————

WEEKLY

*Scripture is God breathed and true.
When we memorize it, we carry the good
news of Jesus with us wherever we go.*

This week we will memorize John 1:2.
In this verse John reaffirms that Jesus is
God by proclaiming that He has always
existed. His life did not begin with His birth
on earth, but instead He has always
been present as God, even at creation.

TRUTH

In the beginning was the Word, and the Word was with God, and the Word was God. He was with God in the beginning. All things were created through him, and apart from him not one thing was created that has been created. In him was life, and that life was the light of men. That light shines in the darkness, and yet the darkness did not overcome it.

JOHN 1:1–5

See tips for memorizing Scripture on page 164.

"YOU WILL KNOW THE TRUTH, AND THE

TRUTH WILL SET YOU FREE." —JOHN 8:32

DAY 15

THE SON SETS YOU FREE

WEEK 03

John 8:31–59

³¹ Then Jesus said to the Jews who had believed him, "If you continue in my word, you really are my disciples. ³² You will know the truth, and the truth will set you free."

³³ "We are descendants of Abraham," they answered him, "and we have never been enslaved to anyone. How can you say, 'You will become free'?"

³⁴ Jesus responded, "Truly I tell you, everyone who commits sin is a slave of sin. ³⁵ A slave does not remain in the household forever, but a son does remain forever.

³⁶ So if the Son sets you free, you really will be free.

³⁷ I know you are descendants of Abraham, but you are trying to kill me because my word has no place among you. ³⁸ I speak what I have seen in the presence of the Father; so then, you do what you have heard from your father."

³⁹ "Our father is Abraham," they replied.

"If you were Abraham's children," Jesus told them, "you would do what Abraham did. ⁴⁰ But now you are trying to kill me, a man who has told you the truth that I heard from God. Abraham did not do this. ⁴¹ You're doing what your father does."

"We weren't born of sexual immorality," they said. "We have one Father—God."

⁴² Jesus said to them, "If God were your Father, you would love me, because I came from God and I am here. For I didn't come on my own, but he sent me. ⁴³ Why don't you understand what I say? Because you cannot listen to my word. ⁴⁴ You are of your father the devil, and you want to carry out your father's desires. He was a murderer from the beginning and does not stand in the truth, because there is no truth in him. When he tells a lie, he speaks from his own nature, because he is a liar and the father of lies. ⁴⁵ Yet because I tell the truth, you do not believe me. ⁴⁶ Who among you can convict me of sin? If I am telling the truth, why don't you believe me? ⁴⁷ The one who is from God listens to God's words. This is why you don't listen, because you are not from God."

48 The Jews responded to him, "Aren't we right in saying that you're a Samaritan and have a demon?"

49 "I do not have a demon," Jesus answered. "On the contrary, I honor my Father and you dishonor me. 50 I do not seek my own glory; there is one who seeks it and judges. 51 Truly I tell you, if anyone keeps my word, he will never see death."

52 Then the Jews said, "Now we know you have a demon. Abraham died and so did the prophets. You say, 'If anyone keeps my word, he will never taste death.' 53 Are you greater than our father Abraham who died? And the prophets died. Who do you claim to be?"

54 "If I glorify myself," Jesus answered, "my glory is nothing. My Father—about whom you say, 'He is our God'—he is the one who glorifies me. 55 You do not know him, but I know him. If I were to say I don't know him, I would be a liar like you. But I do know him, and I keep his word. 56 Your father Abraham rejoiced to see my day; he saw it and was glad."

57 The Jews replied, "You aren't fifty years old yet, and you've seen Abraham?"

58 Jesus said to them, "Truly I tell you, before Abraham was, I am."

59 So they picked up stones to throw at him. But Jesus was hidden and went out of the temple.

💛 GOING DEEPER

Romans 6:15–18

FROM SLAVES OF SIN TO SLAVES OF GOD

15 What then? Should we sin because we are not under the law but under grace? Absolutely not! 16 Don't you know that if you offer yourselves to someone as obedient slaves, you are slaves of that one you obey—either of sin leading to death or of obedience leading to righteousness? 17 But thank God that, although you used to be slaves of sin, you obeyed from the heart that pattern of teaching to which you were handed over,

18 **and having been set free from sin, you became enslaved to righteousness.**

Galatians 5:1

For freedom, Christ set us free. Stand firm, then, and don't submit again to a yoke of slavery.

People who interacted with Jesus:	How they responded to Him:	How He engaged with them:

In today's reading there was...

(check all that apply)

○ A miracle

_____

○ An "I am" statement

_____

○ A festival or feast

☐ PASSOVER

☐ FESTIVAL OF TABERNACLES

☐ FESTIVAL OF DEDICATION

☐ OTHER _____

Descriptive details I noticed:

Statements about Jesus's identity:	Statements about Jesus's mission:

WEEK

03

JESUS HEALS THE BLIND

John 9

THE SIXTH SIGN: HEALING A MAN BORN BLIND

¹ As he was passing by, he saw a man blind from birth. ² His disciples asked him, "Rabbi, who sinned, this man or his parents, that he was born blind?"

³ "Neither this man nor his parents sinned," Jesus answered.

"This came about so that God's works might be displayed in him.

⁴ We must do the works of him who sent me while it is day. Night is coming when no one can work. ⁵ As long as I am in the world, I am the light of the world."

⁶ After he said these things he spit on the ground, made some mud from the saliva, and spread the mud on his eyes. ⁷ "Go," he told him, "wash in the pool of Siloam" (which means "Sent"). So he left, washed, and came back seeing.

⁸ His neighbors and those who had seen him before as a beggar said, "Isn't this the one who used to sit begging?" ⁹ Some said, "He's the one." Others were saying, "No, but he looks like him."

He kept saying, "I'm the one."

¹⁰ So they asked him, "Then how were your eyes opened?"

¹¹ He answered, "The man called Jesus made mud, spread it on my eyes, and told me, 'Go to Siloam and wash.' So when I went and washed I received my sight."

¹² "Where is he?" they asked.

"I don't know," he said.

THE HEALED MAN'S TESTIMONY

¹³ They brought the man who used to be blind to the Pharisees. ¹⁴ The day that Jesus made the mud and opened his eyes was a Sabbath. ¹⁵ Then the Pharisees asked him again how he received his sight.

"He put mud on my eyes," he told them. "I washed and I can see."

¹⁶ Some of the Pharisees said, "This man is not from God, because he doesn't keep the Sabbath." But others were saying, "How can a sinful man perform such signs?" And there was a division among them.

¹⁷ Again they asked the blind man, "What do you say about him, since he opened your eyes?"

"He's a prophet," he said.

¹⁸ The Jews did not believe this about him—that he was blind and received sight—until they summoned the parents of the one who had received his sight.

¹⁹ They asked them, "Is this your son, the one you say was born blind? How then does he now see?"

²⁰ "We know this is our son and that he was born blind," his parents answered. ²¹ "But we don't know how he now sees, and we don't know who opened his eyes. Ask him; he's of age. He will speak for himself." ²² His parents said these things because they were afraid of the Jews, since the Jews had already agreed that if anyone confessed him as the Messiah, he would be banned from the synagogue. ²³ This is why his parents said, "He's of age; ask him."

²⁴ So a second time they summoned the man who had been blind and told him, "Give glory to God. We know that this man is a sinner."

25 He answered, "Whether or not he's a sinner, I don't know. One thing I do know: I was blind, and now I can see!"

26 Then they asked him, "What did he do to you? How did he open your eyes?"

27 "I already told you," he said, "and you didn't listen. Why do you want to hear it again? You don't want to become his disciples too, do you?"

28 They ridiculed him: "You're that man's disciple, but we're Moses's disciples. 29 We know that God has spoken to Moses. But this man—we don't know where he's from."

30 "This is an amazing thing!" the man told them. "You don't know where he is from, and yet he opened my eyes. 31 We know that God doesn't listen to sinners, but if anyone is God-fearing and does his will, he listens to him. 32 Throughout history no one has ever heard of someone opening the eyes of a person born blind. 33 If this man were not from God, he wouldn't be able to do anything."

34 "You were born entirely in sin," they replied, "and are you trying to teach us?" Then they threw him out.

SPIRITUAL BLINDNESS

35 Jesus heard that they had thrown the man out, and when he found him, he asked, "Do you believe in the Son of Man?"

36 "Who is he, Sir, that I may believe in him?" he asked.

37 Jesus answered, "You have seen him; in fact, he is the one speaking with you."

38 "I believe, Lord!" he said, and he worshiped him.

39 Jesus said, "I came into this world for judgment, in order that those who do not see will see and those who do see will become blind."

40 Some of the Pharisees who were with him heard these things and asked him, "We aren't blind too, are we?"

41 "If you were blind," Jesus told them, "you wouldn't have sin. But now that you say, 'We see,' your sin remains."

🔖 GOING DEEPER

Genesis 2:7

Then the LORD God formed the man out of the dust from the ground and breathed the breath of life into his nostrils, and the man became a living being.

Romans 1:18–20

THE GUILT OF THE GENTILE WORLD

18 For God's wrath is revealed from heaven against all godlessness and unrighteousness of people who by their unrighteousness suppress the truth, 19 since what can be known about God is evident among them, because God has shown it to them. 20 For his invisible attributes, that is, his eternal power and divine nature, have been clearly seen since the creation of the world, being understood through what he has made. As a result, people are without excuse.

People who interacted with Jesus:	How they responded to Him:	How He engaged with them:

In today's reading there was...
(check all that apply)

○ A miracle

_____

○ An "I am" statement

_____

○ A festival or feast

☐ PASSOVER

☐ FESTIVAL OF TABERNACLES

☐ FESTIVAL OF DEDICATION

☐ OTHER _____

Descriptive details I noticed:

Statements about Jesus's identity:	Statements about Jesus's mission:

THE GOOD

DAY 17

WEEK 03

SHEPHERD

John 10

THE GOOD SHEPHERD

1 "Truly I tell you, anyone who doesn't enter the sheep pen by the gate but climbs in some other way is a thief and a robber. 2 The one who enters by the gate is the shepherd of the sheep. 3 The gatekeeper opens it for him, and the sheep hear his voice. He calls his own sheep by name and leads them out. 4 When he has brought all his own outside, he goes ahead of them. The sheep follow him because they know his voice. 5 They will never follow a stranger; instead they will run away from him, because they don't know the voice of strangers." 6 Jesus gave them this figure of speech, but they did not understand what he was telling them.

7 Jesus said again, "Truly I tell you, I am the gate for the sheep. 8 All who came before me are thieves and robbers, but the sheep didn't listen to them. 9 I am the gate. If anyone enters by me, he will be saved and will come in and go out and find pasture. 10 A thief comes only to steal and kill and destroy.

I have come so that they may have life and have it in abundance.

11 "I am the good shepherd. The good shepherd lays down his life for the sheep. 12 The hired hand, since he is not the shepherd and doesn't own the sheep, leaves them and runs away when he sees a wolf coming. The wolf then snatches and scatters them. 13 This happens because he is a hired hand and doesn't care about the sheep.

14 "I am the good shepherd. I know my own, and my own know me, 15 just as the Father knows me, and I know the Father. I lay down my life for the sheep. 16 But I have other sheep that are not from this sheep pen; I must bring them also, and they will listen to my voice. Then there will be one flock, one shepherd. 17 This is why the Father loves me, because I lay down my life so that I may take it up again. 18 No one takes it from me, but I lay it down on my own. I have the right to lay it down, and I have the right to take it up again. I have received this command from my Father."

19 Again the Jews were divided because of these words. 20 Many of them were saying, "He has a demon and he's crazy. Why do you listen to him?" 21 Others were saying, "These aren't the words of someone who is demon-possessed. Can a demon open the eyes of the blind?"

JESUS AT THE FESTIVAL OF DEDICATION

22 Then the Festival of Dedication took place in Jerusalem, and it was winter. 23 Jesus was walking in the temple in Solomon's Colonnade. 24 The Jews surrounded him and asked, "How long are you going to keep us in suspense? If you are the Messiah, tell us plainly."

25 "I did tell you and you don't believe," Jesus answered them. "The works that I do in my Father's name testify about me. 26 But you don't believe because you are not of my sheep. 27 My sheep hear my voice, I know them, and they follow me. 28 I give them eternal life, and they will never perish. No one will snatch them out of my hand. 29 My Father, who has given them to me, is greater than all. No one is able to snatch them out of the Father's hand. 30 I and the Father are one."

RENEWED EFFORTS TO STONE JESUS

31 Again the Jews picked up rocks to stone him.

32 Jesus replied, "I have shown you many good works from the Father. For which of these works are you stoning me?"

33 "We aren't stoning you for a good work," the Jews answered, "but for blasphemy, because you—being a man—make yourself God."

34 Jesus answered them, "Isn't it written in your law, I said, you are gods? 35 If he called those to whom the word of God came 'gods'—and the Scripture cannot be broken— 36 do you say, 'You are blaspheming' to the one the Father set apart and sent into the world, because I said: I am the Son of God? 37 If I am not doing my Father's works, don't believe me. 38 But if I am doing them and you don't believe me, believe

the works. This way you will know and understand that the Father is in me and I in the Father." ³⁹ Then they were trying again to seize him, but he escaped their grasp.

MANY BEYOND THE JORDAN BELIEVE IN JESUS

⁴⁰ So he departed again across the Jordan to the place where John had been baptizing earlier, and he remained there. ⁴¹ Many came to him and said, "John never did a sign, but everything John said about this man was true." ⁴² And many believed in him there.

🌱 GOING DEEPER

Numbers 27:16–17

¹⁶ May the Lord, the God who gives breath to all, appoint a man over the community ¹⁷ who will go out before them and come back in before them, and who will bring them out and bring them in, so that the Lord's community won't be like sheep without a shepherd.

Psalm 23:1–4

THE GOOD SHEPHERD

A psalm of David.

¹ The Lord is my shepherd;
I have what I need.

² He lets me lie down in green pastures;
he leads me beside quiet waters.
³ He renews my life;
he leads me along the right paths
for his name's sake.
⁴ Even when I go through the darkest valley,
I fear no danger,
for you are with me;
your rod and your staff—they comfort me.

Micah 2:12–13

THE REMNANT REGATHERED

¹² "I will indeed gather all of you, Jacob;
I will collect the remnant of Israel.

**I will bring them together
like sheep in a pen,
like a flock in the middle
of its pasture.**

It will be noisy with people.
¹³ One who breaks open the way
will advance before them;
they will break out, pass through the
city gate,
and leave by it.
Their King will pass through before them,
the Lord as their leader."

People who interacted with Jesus:	How they responded to Him:	How He engaged with them:

In today's reading there was...

(check all that apply)

○ A miracle

_____

○ An "I am" statement

_____

○ A festival or feast

☐ PASSOVER

☐ FESTIVAL OF TABERNACLES

☐ FESTIVAL OF DEDICATION

☐ OTHER _____

Descriptive details I noticed:

Statements about Jesus's identity:	Statements about Jesus's mission:

THE RESURRECTION AND THE LIFE

WEEK 03

LAZARUS DIES AT BETHANY

¹ Now a man was sick, Lazarus from Bethany, the village of Mary and her sister Martha. ² Mary was the one who anointed the Lord with perfume and wiped his feet with her hair, and it was her brother Lazarus who was sick. ³ So the sisters sent a message to him: "Lord, the one you love is sick."

⁴ When Jesus heard it, he said,

> "This sickness will not end in death but is for the glory of God, so that the Son of God may be glorified through it."

⁵ Now Jesus loved Martha, her sister, and Lazarus. ⁶ So when he heard that he was sick, he stayed two more days in the place where he was. ⁷ Then after that, he said to the disciples, "Let's go to Judea again."

⁸ "Rabbi," the disciples told him, "just now the Jews tried to stone you, and you're going there again?"

⁹ "Aren't there twelve hours in a day?" Jesus answered. "If anyone walks during the day, he doesn't stumble, because he sees the light of this world. ¹⁰ But if anyone walks during the night, he does stumble, because the light is not in him."

¹¹ He said this, and then he told them, "Our friend Lazarus has fallen asleep, but I'm on my way to wake him up."

¹² Then the disciples said to him, "Lord, if he has fallen asleep, he will get well."

¹³ Jesus, however, was speaking about his death, but they thought he was speaking about natural sleep. ¹⁴ So Jesus then told them plainly, "Lazarus has died. ¹⁵ I'm glad for you that I wasn't there so that you may believe. But let's go to him."

¹⁶ Then Thomas (called "Twin") said to his fellow disciples, "Let's go too so that we may die with him."

THE RESURRECTION AND THE LIFE

¹⁷ When Jesus arrived, he found that Lazarus had already been in the tomb four days. ¹⁸ Bethany was near Jerusalem (less than two miles away). ¹⁹ Many of the Jews had come to Martha and Mary to comfort them about their brother.

²⁰ As soon as Martha heard that Jesus was coming, she went to meet him, but Mary remained seated in the house. ²¹ Then Martha said to Jesus, "Lord, if you had been here, my brother wouldn't have died. ²² Yet even now I know that whatever you ask from God, God will give you."

²³ "Your brother will rise again," Jesus told her.

²⁴ Martha said to him, "I know that he will rise again in the resurrection at the last day."

²⁵ Jesus said to her, "I am the resurrection and the life. The one who believes in me, even if he dies, will live. ²⁶ Everyone who lives and believes in me will never die. Do you believe this?"

²⁷ "Yes, Lord," she told him, "I believe you are the Messiah, the Son of God, who comes into the world."

JESUS SHARES THE SORROW OF DEATH

²⁸ Having said this, she went back and called her sister Mary, saying in private, "The Teacher is here and is calling for you."

²⁹ As soon as Mary heard this, she got up quickly and went to him. ³⁰ Jesus had not yet come into the village but was still in the place where Martha had met him. ³¹ The Jews who were with her in the house consoling her saw that Mary got up quickly and went out. They followed her, supposing that she was going to the tomb to cry there.

³² As soon as Mary came to where Jesus was and saw him, she fell at his feet and told him, "Lord, if you had been here, my brother wouldn't have died!"

³³ When Jesus saw her crying, and the Jews who had come with her crying, he was deeply moved in his spirit and troubled. ³⁴ "Where have you put him?" he asked.

"Lord," they told him, "come and see."

³⁵ Jesus wept.

³⁶ So the Jews said, "See how he loved him!" ³⁷ But some of them said, "Couldn't he who opened the blind man's eyes also have kept this man from dying?"

THE SEVENTH SIGN: RAISING LAZARUS FROM THE DEAD

³⁸ Then Jesus, deeply moved again, came to the tomb. It was a cave, and a stone was lying against it. ³⁹ "Remove the stone," Jesus said.

Martha, the dead man's sister, told him, "Lord, there is already a stench because he has been dead four days."

⁴⁰ Jesus said to her, "Didn't I tell you that if you believed you would see the glory of God?"

⁴¹ So they removed the stone. Then Jesus raised his eyes and said, "Father, I thank you that you heard me. ⁴² I know that you always hear me, but because of the crowd standing here I said this, so that they may believe you sent me." ⁴³ After he said this, he shouted with a loud voice, "Lazarus, come out!" ⁴⁴ The dead man came out bound hand and foot with linen strips and with his face wrapped in a cloth. Jesus said to them, "Unwrap him and let him go."

THE PLOT TO KILL JESUS

⁴⁵ Therefore, many of the Jews who came to Mary and saw what he did believed in him. ⁴⁶ But some of them went to the Pharisees and told them what Jesus had done.

⁴⁷ So the chief priests and the Pharisees convened the Sanhedrin and were saying, "What are we going to do since this man is doing many signs? ⁴⁸ If we let him go on like this, everyone will believe in him, and the Romans will come and take away both our place and our nation."

⁴⁹ One of them, Caiaphas, who was high priest that year, said to them, "You know nothing at all! ⁵⁰ You're not considering that it is to your advantage that one man should die for the people rather than the whole nation perish." ⁵¹ He did not say this on his own, but being high priest that year he prophesied that Jesus was going to die for the

nation, [52] and not for the nation only, but also to unite the scattered children of God. [53] So from that day on they plotted to kill him.

[54] Jesus therefore no longer walked openly among the Jews but departed from there to the countryside near the wilderness, to a town called Ephraim, and he stayed there with the disciples.

🛡 GOING DEEPER

Daniel 12:2–3

[2] Many who sleep in the dust
of the earth will awake,
some to eternal life,
and some to disgrace and eternal contempt.
[3] Those who have insight will shine
like the bright expanse of the heavens,
and those who lead many to righteousness,
like the stars forever and ever.

1 Corinthians 15:12–19

RESURRECTION ESSENTIAL TO THE FAITH

[12] Now if Christ is proclaimed as raised from the dead, how can some of you say, "There is no resurrection of the dead"? [13] If there is no resurrection of the dead, then not even Christ has been raised; [14] and if Christ has not been raised, then our proclamation is in vain, and so is your faith. [15] Moreover, we are found to be false witnesses about God, because we have testified wrongly about God that he raised up Christ—whom he did not raise up, if in fact the dead are not raised. [16] For if the dead are not raised, not even Christ has been raised. [17] And if Christ has not been raised, your faith is worthless; you are still in your sins. [18] Those, then, who have fallen asleep in Christ have also perished. [19] If we have put our hope in Christ for this life only, we should be pitied more than anyone.

People who interacted with Jesus:	How they responded to Him:	How He engaged with them:

In today's reading there was...
(check all that apply)

○ A miracle

_____

○ An "I am" statement

_____

○ A festival or feast

☐ PASSOVER

☐ FESTIVAL OF TABERNACLES

☐ FESTIVAL OF DEDICATION

☐ OTHER _____

Descriptive details I noticed:

Statements about Jesus's identity:	Statements about Jesus's mission:

THE ANOINTED ONE

WEEK 03

John 11:55–57

⁵⁵ Now the Jewish Passover was near, and many went up to Jerusalem from the country to purify themselves before the Passover. ⁵⁶ They were looking for Jesus and asking one another as they stood in the temple, "What do you think? He won't come to the festival, will he?" ⁵⁷ The chief priests and the Pharisees had given orders that if anyone knew where he was, he should report it so that they could arrest him.

John 12:1–36

THE ANOINTING AT BETHANY

¹ Six days before the Passover, Jesus came to Bethany where Lazarus was, the one Jesus had raised from the dead. ² So they gave a dinner for him there; Martha was serving them, and Lazarus was one of those reclining at the table with him. ³ Then Mary took a pound of perfume, pure and expensive nard, anointed Jesus's feet, and wiped his feet with her hair. So the house was filled with the fragrance of the perfume.

⁴ Then one of his disciples, Judas Iscariot (who was about to betray him), said, ⁵ "Why wasn't this perfume sold for three hundred denarii and given to the poor?" ⁶ He didn't say this because he cared about the poor but because he was a thief. He was in charge of the money-bag and would steal part of what was put in it.

⁷ Jesus answered, "Leave her alone; she has kept it for the day of my burial. ⁸ For you always have the poor with you, but you do not always have me."

THE DECISION TO KILL LAZARUS

⁹ Then a large crowd of the Jews learned he was there. They came not only because of Jesus but also to see Lazarus, the one he had raised from the dead. ¹⁰ But the chief priests had decided to kill Lazarus also, ¹¹ because he was the reason many of the Jews were deserting them and believing in Jesus.

THE TRIUMPHAL ENTRY

¹² The next day, when the large crowd that had come to the festival heard that Jesus was coming to Jerusalem, ¹³ they took palm branches and went out to meet him. They kept shouting:

> *"Hosanna!*
> Blessed is he who comes in the name of the Lord—the
> King of Israel!"

¹⁴ Jesus found a young donkey and sat on it, just as it is written:

> ¹⁵ Do not be afraid,
> Daughter Zion. Look, your King is coming,
> sitting on a donkey's colt.

¹⁶ His disciples did not understand these things at first. However, when Jesus was glorified, then they remembered that these things had been written about him and that they had done these things to him.

¹⁷ Meanwhile, the crowd, which had been with him when he called Lazarus out of the tomb and raised him from the dead, continued to testify. ¹⁸ This is also why the crowd met him, because they heard he had done this sign. ¹⁹ Then the Pharisees said to one another, "You see? You've accomplished nothing. Look, the world has gone after him!"

JESUS PREDICTS HIS CRUCIFIXION

²⁰ Now some Greeks were among those who went up to worship at the festival. ²¹ So they came to Philip, who was from Bethsaida in Galilee, and requested of him, "Sir, we want to see Jesus." ²² Philip went and told Andrew; then Andrew and Philip went and told Jesus.

²³ Jesus replied to them, "The hour has come for the Son of Man to be glorified. ²⁴ Truly I tell you, unless a grain of

wheat falls to the ground and dies, it remains by itself. But if it dies, it produces much fruit. ²⁵ The one who loves his life will lose it, and the one who hates his life in this world will keep it for eternal life. ²⁶ If anyone serves me, he must follow me. Where I am, there my servant also will be. If anyone serves me, the Father will honor him.

²⁷ "Now my soul is troubled. What should I say—Father, save me from this hour? But that is why I came to this hour. ²⁸ Father, glorify your name."

Then a voice came from heaven: "I have glorified it, and I will glorify it again."

²⁹ The crowd standing there heard it and said it was thunder. Others said, "An angel has spoken to him."

³⁰ Jesus responded, "This voice came, not for me, but for you. ³¹ Now is the judgment of this world. Now the ruler of this world will be cast out. ³² As for me, if I am lifted up from the earth I will draw all people to myself." ³³ He said this to indicate what kind of death he was about to die.

³⁴ Then the crowd replied to him, "We have heard from the law that the Messiah will remain forever. So how can you say, 'The Son of Man must be lifted up'? Who is this Son of Man?"

³⁵ Jesus answered, "The light will be with you only a little longer. Walk while you have the light so that darkness doesn't overtake you. The one who walks in darkness doesn't know where he's going. ³⁶ While you have the light, believe in the light so that you may become children of light." Jesus said this, then went away and hid from them.

⬕ GOING DEEPER

Exodus 30:23–33

²³ "Take for yourself the finest spices: 12½ pounds of liquid myrrh, half as much (6¼ pounds) of fragrant cinnamon, 6¼ pounds of fragrant cane, ²⁴ 12½ pounds of cassia (by the sanctuary shekel), and a gallon of olive oil. ²⁵ Prepare from these a holy anointing oil, a scented blend, the work of a perfumer; it will be holy anointing oil.

²⁶ "With it you are to anoint the tent of meeting, the ark of the testimony, ²⁷ the table with all its utensils, the lampstand with its utensils, the altar of incense, ²⁸ the altar of burnt offering with all its utensils, and the basin with its stand. ²⁹ Consecrate them and they will be especially holy. Whatever touches them will be consecrated. ³⁰ Anoint Aaron and his sons and consecrate them to serve me as priests.

³¹ "Tell the Israelites: This will be my holy anointing oil throughout your generations. ³² It must not be used for ordinary anointing on a person's body, and you must not make anything like it using its formula. It is holy, and it must be holy to you. ³³ Anyone who blends something like it or puts some of it on an unauthorized person must be cut off from his people."

Isaiah 61:1–3

MESSIAH'S JUBILEE

¹ The Spirit of the Lord God is on me,
because the Lord has anointed me
to bring good news to the poor.

He has sent me to heal the brokenhearted, to proclaim liberty to the captives and freedom to the prisoners;

² to proclaim the year of the Lord's favor,
and the day of our God's vengeance;
to comfort all who mourn,
³ to provide for those who mourn in Zion;
to give them a crown of beauty instead of ashes,
festive oil instead of mourning,
and splendid clothes instead of despair.
And they will be called righteous trees,
planted by the Lord
to glorify him.

People who interacted with Jesus:	How they responded to Him:	How He engaged with them:

In today's reading there was...

(check all that apply)

○ A miracle

_____

○ An "I am" statement

_____

○ A festival or feast

☐ PASSOVER

☐ FESTIVAL OF TABERNACLES

☐ FESTIVAL OF DEDICATION

☐ OTHER _____

Descriptive details I noticed:

Statements about Jesus's identity:	Statements about Jesus's mission:

GRACE

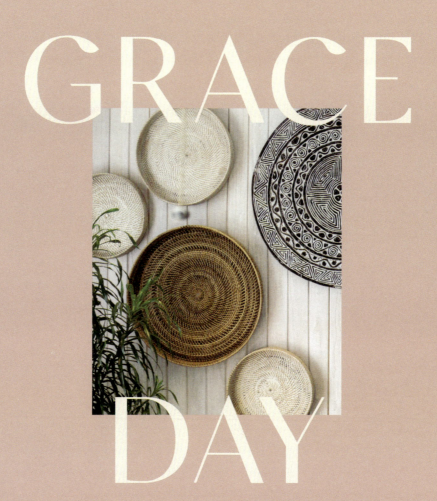

DAY

Take this day
to catch up on
your reading,
pray, and rest in
the presence
of the Lord.

For freedom,
Christ set us free.
Stand firm, then,
and don't submit
again to a yoke
of slavery.

GALATIANS 5:1 ————————————————————————

WEEKLY

*Scripture is God breathed and true.
When we memorize it, we carry the good
news of Jesus with us wherever we go.*

This week we will continue memorizing
John's prologue. In John 1:3, John
emphasizes Jesus's divine nature by
pointing to His active role in creation.

TRUTH

In the beginning was the Word, and the Word was with God, and the Word was God. He was with God in the beginning. All things were created through him, and apart from him not one thing was created that has been created. In him was life, and that life was the light of men. That light shines in the darkness, and yet the darkness did not overcome it.

JOHN 1:1–5

See tips for memorizing Scripture on page 164.

WEEK

THE FULFILLMENT OF PROPHECIES

04

John 12:37–50

ISAIAH'S PROPHECIES FULFILLED

[37] Even though he had performed so many signs in their presence, they did not believe in him. [38] This was to fulfill the word of Isaiah the prophet, who said:

> Lord, who has believed our message?
> And to whom has the arm of the Lord been revealed?

[39] This is why they were unable to believe, because Isaiah also said:

> [40] He has blinded their eyes
> and hardened their hearts,
> so that they would not see with their eyes
> or understand with their hearts,
> and turn,
> and I would heal them.

[41] Isaiah said these things because he saw his glory and spoke about him.

[42] Nevertheless, many did believe in him even among the rulers, but because of the Pharisees they did not confess him, so that they would not be banned from the synagogue.

[43] For they loved human praise more than praise from God.

A SUMMARY OF JESUS'S MISSION

[44] Jesus cried out, "The one who believes in me believes not in me, but in him who sent me. [45] And the one who sees me sees him who sent me. [46] I have come as light into the world, so that everyone who believes in me would not remain in darkness. [47] If anyone hears my words and doesn't keep them, I do not judge him; for I did not come to judge the world but to save the world. [48] The one who rejects me and doesn't receive my sayings has this as his judge: The word I have spoken will judge him on the last day. [49] For I have not spoken on my own, but the Father himself who sent me has given me a command to say everything I have said. [50] I know that his command is eternal life. So the things that I speak, I speak just as the Father has told me."

Isaiah 53:1–6

1 Who has believed what we have heard?
And to whom has the arm of the Lᴏʀᴅ been revealed?
2 He grew up before him like a young plant
and like a root out of dry ground.
He didn't have an impressive form
or majesty that we should look at him,
no appearance that we should desire him.
3 He was despised and rejected by men,
a man of suffering who knew what sickness was.
He was like someone people turned away from;
he was despised, and we didn't value him.

4 Yet he himself bore our sicknesses,
and he carried our pains;
but we in turn regarded him stricken,
struck down by God, and afflicted.
5 But he was pierced because of our rebellion,
crushed because of our iniquities;
punishment for our peace was on him,
and we are healed by his wounds.
6 We all went astray like sheep;
we all have turned to our own way;
and the Lᴏʀᴅ has punished him
for the iniquity of us all.

Luke 11:29–32

THE SIGN OF JONAH

29 As the crowds were increasing, he began saying, "This generation is an evil generation. It demands a sign, but no sign will be given to it except the sign of Jonah. 30 For just as Jonah became a sign to the people of Nineveh, so also the Son of Man will be to this generation. 31 The queen of the south will rise up at the judgment with the men of this generation and condemn them, because she came from the ends of the earth to hear the wisdom of Solomon, and look—something greater than Solomon is here. 32 The men of Nineveh will stand up at the judgment with this generation and condemn it, because they repented at Jonah's preaching, and look—something greater than Jonah is here."

People who interacted with Jesus:	How they responded to Him:	How He engaged with them:

In today's reading there was...

(check all that apply)

O A miracle

_____

O An "I am" statement

_____

O A festival or feast

☐ PASSOVER

☐ FESTIVAL OF TABERNACLES

☐ FESTIVAL OF DEDICATION

☐ OTHER _____

Descriptive details I noticed:

Statements about Jesus's identity:	Statements about Jesus's mission:

HAVING LOVED HIS OWN WHO WERE IN THE WORLD.

HE LOVED THEM TO THE END. —JOHN 13:1

JESUS DISPLAYS HIS LOVE

WEEK 04

John 13

JESUS WASHES HIS DISCIPLES' FEET

[1] Before the Passover Festival, Jesus knew that his hour had come to depart from this world to the Father. Having loved his own who were in the world, he loved them to the end.

[2] Now when it was time for supper, the devil had already put it into the heart of Judas, Simon Iscariot's son, to betray him. [3] Jesus knew that the Father had given everything into his hands, that he had come from God, and that he was going back to God. [4] So he got up from supper, laid aside his outer clothing, took a towel, and tied it around himself. [5] Next, he poured water into a basin and began to wash his disciples' feet and to dry them with the towel tied around him.

[6] He came to Simon Peter, who asked him, "Lord, are you going to wash my feet?"

[7] Jesus answered him, "What I'm doing you don't realize now, but afterward you will understand."

[8] "You will never wash my feet," Peter said.

Jesus replied, "If I don't wash you, you have no part with me."

[9] Simon Peter said to him, "Lord, not only my feet, but also my hands and my head."

[10] "One who has bathed," Jesus told him, "doesn't need to wash anything except his feet, but he is completely clean. You are clean, but not all of you." [11] For he knew who would betray him. This is why he said, "Not all of you are clean."

THE MEANING OF FOOT WASHING

[12] When Jesus had washed their feet and put on his outer clothing, he reclined again and said to them, "Do you know what I have done for you? [13] You call me Teacher and Lord—and you are speaking rightly, since that is what I am. [14] So if I, your Lord and Teacher, have washed your feet, you also ought to wash one another's feet. [15] For I have given you an example, that you also should do just as I have done for you.

[16] "Truly I tell you, a servant is not greater than his master, and a messenger is not greater than the one who sent him. [17] If you know these things, you are blessed if you do them.

[18] "I'm not speaking about all of you; I know those I have chosen. But the Scripture must be fulfilled: The one who eats my bread has raised his heel against me. [19] I am telling you now before it happens, so that when it does happen you will believe that I am he. [20] Truly I tell you, whoever receives anyone I send receives me, and the one who receives me receives him who sent me."

JUDAS'S BETRAYAL PREDICTED

[21] When Jesus had said this, he was troubled in his spirit and testified, "Truly I tell you, one of you will betray me."

[22] The disciples started looking at one another—uncertain which one he was speaking about. [23] One of his disciples, the one Jesus loved, was reclining close beside Jesus. [24] Simon Peter motioned to him to find out who it was he was talking about. [25] So he leaned back against Jesus and asked him, "Lord, who is it?"

[26] Jesus replied, "He's the one I give the piece of bread to after I have dipped it." When he had dipped the bread, he gave it to Judas, Simon Iscariot's son. [27] After Judas ate the piece of bread, Satan entered him. So Jesus told him, "What you're doing, do quickly."

[28] None of those reclining at the table knew why he said this to him. [29] Since Judas kept the money-bag, some thought that Jesus was telling him, "Buy what we need for the festival," or that he should give something to the poor. [30] After receiving the piece of bread, he immediately left. And it was night.

THE NEW COMMAND

³¹ When he had left, Jesus said, "Now the Son of Man is glorified, and God is glorified in him. ³² If God is glorified in him, God will also glorify him in himself and will glorify him at once. ³³ Little children, I am with you a little while longer. You will look for me, and just as I told the Jews, so now I tell you, 'Where I am going, you cannot come.'

³⁴ "I give you a new command: Love one another. Just as I have loved you, you are also to love one another. ³⁵ By this everyone will know that you are my disciples, if you love one another."

PETER'S DENIALS PREDICTED

³⁶ "Lord," Simon Peter said to him, "where are you going?"

Jesus answered, "Where I am going you cannot follow me now, but you will follow later."

³⁷ "Lord," Peter asked, "why can't I follow you now? I will lay down my life for you."

³⁸ Jesus replied, "Will you lay down your life for me? Truly I tell you, a rooster will not crow until you have denied me three times."

◖ GOING DEEPER

Isaiah 42:1

"This is my servant; I strengthen him,
this is my chosen one; I delight in him.
I have put my Spirit on him;
he will bring justice to the nations."

Mark 10:45

"For even the Son of Man did not come to be served, but to serve, and to give his life as a ransom for many."

Philippians 2:5–11

CHRIST'S HUMILITY AND EXALTATION

⁵ Adopt the same attitude as that of Christ Jesus,

⁶ who, existing in the form of God,
did not consider equality with God
as something to be exploited.
⁷ Instead he emptied himself
by assuming the form of a servant,
taking on the likeness of humanity.
And when he had come as a man,
⁸ he humbled himself by becoming obedient
to the point of death—
even to death on a cross.
⁹ For this reason God highly exalted him
and gave him the name
that is above every name,
¹⁰ so that at the name of Jesus
every knee will bow—
in heaven and on earth
and under the earth—
¹¹ and every tongue will confess
that Jesus Christ is Lord,
to the glory of God the Father.

People who interacted with Jesus:	How they responded to Him:	How He engaged with them:

In today's reading there was...

(check all that apply)

○ A miracle

_____

○ An "I am" statement

_____

○ A festival or feast

☐ PASSOVER

☐ FESTIVAL OF TABERNACLES

☐ FESTIVAL OF DEDICATION

☐ OTHER _____

Descriptive details I noticed:

Statements about Jesus's identity:	Statements about Jesus's mission:

THE WAY, THE TRUTH, AND THE LIFE

—

John 14

¹ "Don't let your heart be troubled. Believe in God; believe also in me. ² In my Father's house are many rooms. If it were not so, would I have told you that I am going to prepare a place for you? ³ If I go away and prepare a place for you, I will come again and take you to myself, so that where I am you may be also. ⁴ You know the way to where I am going."

⁵ "Lord," Thomas said, "we don't know where you're going. How can we know the way?"

⁶ Jesus told him, "I am the way, the truth, and the life. No one comes to the Father except through me. ⁷ If you know me, you will also know my Father. From now on you do know him and have seen him."

JESUS REVEALS THE FATHER

⁸ "Lord," said Philip, "show us the Father, and that's enough for us."

⁹ Jesus said to him, "Have I been among you all this time and you do not know me, Philip? The one who has seen me has seen the Father. How can you say, 'Show us the Father'? ¹⁰ Don't you believe that I am in the Father and the Father is in me? The words I speak to you I do not speak on my own. The Father who lives in me does his works. ¹¹ Believe me that I am in the Father and the Father is in me. Otherwise, believe because of the works themselves.

PRAYING IN JESUS'S NAME

¹² "Truly I tell you, the one who believes in me will also do the works that I do. And he will do even greater works than these, because I am going to the Father. ¹³ Whatever you ask in my name, I will do it so that the Father may be glorified in the Son. ¹⁴ If you ask me anything in my name, I will do it.

ANOTHER COUNSELOR PROMISED

¹⁵ "If you love me, you will keep my commands. ¹⁶ And I will ask the Father, and he will give you another Counselor to be with you forever. ¹⁷ He is the Spirit of truth. The world is unable to receive him because it doesn't see him or know him. But you do know him, because he remains with you and will be in you.

THE FATHER, THE SON, AND THE HOLY SPIRIT

¹⁸ "I will not leave you as orphans; I am coming to you. ¹⁹ In a little while the world will no longer see me, but you will see me. Because I live, you will live too. ²⁰ On that day you will know that I am in my Father, you are in me, and I am in you. ²¹ The one who has my commands and keeps them is the one who loves me. And the one who loves me will be loved by my Father. I also will love him and will reveal myself to him."

²² Judas (not Iscariot) said to him, "Lord, how is it you're going to reveal yourself to us and not to the world?"

²³ Jesus answered, "If anyone loves me, he will keep my word. My Father will love him, and we will come to him and make our home with him. ²⁴ The one who doesn't love me will not keep my words. The word that you hear is not mine but is from the Father who sent me.

²⁵ "I have spoken these things to you while I remain with you.

²⁶ **But the Counselor, the Holy Spirit, whom the Father will send in my name, will teach you all things and remind you of everything I have told you.**

JESUS'S GIFT OF PEACE

²⁷ "Peace I leave with you. My peace I give to you. I do not give to you as the world gives. Don't let your heart be troubled or fearful. ²⁸ You have heard me tell you, 'I am going away and I am coming to you.' If you loved me, you would rejoice that I am going to the Father, because the Father is greater than I. ²⁹ I have told you now before it happens so that when it does happen you may believe. ³⁰ I will not talk with you much longer, because the ruler of

the world is coming. He has no power over me. [31] On the contrary, so that the world may know that I love the Father, I do as the Father commanded me.

"Get up; let's leave this place."

🛡 GOING DEEPER

Isaiah 28:16

Therefore the Lord GOD said:
"Look, I have laid a stone in Zion,
a tested stone,
a precious cornerstone, a sure foundation;
the one who believes will be unshakable."

Matthew 11:25–27

THE SON GIVES KNOWLEDGE AND REST

[25] At that time Jesus said, "I praise you, Father, Lord of heaven and earth, because you have hidden these things from the wise and intelligent and revealed them to infants. [26] Yes, Father, because this was your good pleasure. [27] All things have been entrusted to me by my Father. No one knows the Son except the Father, and no one knows the Father except the Son and anyone to whom the Son desires to reveal him."

Acts 4:12

There is salvation in no one else, for there is no other name under heaven given to people by which we must be saved.

Hebrews 10:19–22

[19] Therefore, brothers and sisters, since we have boldness to enter the sanctuary through the blood of Jesus— [20] he has inaugurated for us a new and living way through the curtain (that is, through his flesh)— [21] and since we have a great high priest over the house of God, [22] let us draw near with a true heart in full assurance of faith, with our hearts sprinkled clean from an evil conscience and our bodies washed in pure water.

People who interacted with Jesus:	How they responded to Him:	How He engaged with them:

In today's reading there was...
(check all that apply)

○ A miracle

_____

○ An "I am" statement

_____

○ A festival or feast

☐ PASSOVER

☐ FESTIVAL OF TABERNACLES

☐ FESTIVAL OF DEDICATION

☐ OTHER _____

Descriptive details I noticed:

Statements about Jesus's identity:	Statements about Jesus's mission:

WITNESSES OF JESUS

Each of the Gospels records how Jesus was put on trial before His death on the cross. The Gospel of John goes even further, structuring the entire account around witness testimony. Throughout the book of John, these witnesses are metaphorically "called to the stand" to testify to Jesus's divinity.

Listed below are some of the witnesses to Jesus's divinity found in John's Gospel.

JOHN THE BAPTIST

This was the one of whom I said, "The one coming after me ranks ahead of me, because he existed before me."

JN 1:15

I saw the Spirit descending from heaven like a dove, and he rested on him. I didn't know him, but he who sent me to baptize with water told me, "The one you see the Spirit descending and resting on—he is the one who baptizes with the Holy Spirit." I have seen and testified that this is the Son of God.

JN 1:32–34

GOD THE FATHER

"The father who sent me has himself testified about me. You have not heard his voice at any time, and you haven't seen his form. You don't have his word residing in you, because you don't believe the one he sent."

JN 5:37–38

"I am the one who testifies about myself, and the father who sent me testifies about me."

JN 8:18

THE SAMARITAN WOMAN

Then the woman left her water jar, went into town, and told the people, "Come, see a man who told me everything I ever did. Could this be the Messiah?"

JN 4:28-29

Now many Samaritans from that town believed in him because of what the woman said when she testified, "He told me everything I ever did."

JN 4:39

JOHN THE APOSTLE

He who saw this has testified so that you also may believe. His testimony is true, and he knows he is telling the truth.

JN 19:35

This is the disciple who testifies to these things and who wrote them down. We know that his testimony is true.

JN 21:24

GOD THE SON, JESUS

"But I have a greater testimony than John's because of the works that the Father has given me to accomplish. These very works I am doing testify about me that the Father has sent me."

JN 5:36

"Even if I testify about myself," Jesus replied. "My testimony is true, because I know where I came from and where I'm going. But you don't know where I come from or where I'm going."

JN 8:14

"The works that I do in my Father's name testify about me."

JN 10:25

GOD THE HOLY SPIRIT

"When the Counselor comes, the one I will send to you from the Father—the Spirit of truth who proceeds from the Father—he will testify about me."

JN 15:26

THE OLD TESTAMENT SCRIPTURES

"You pore over the Scriptures because you think you have eternal life in them, and yet they testify about me."

JN 5:39

THE TRUE

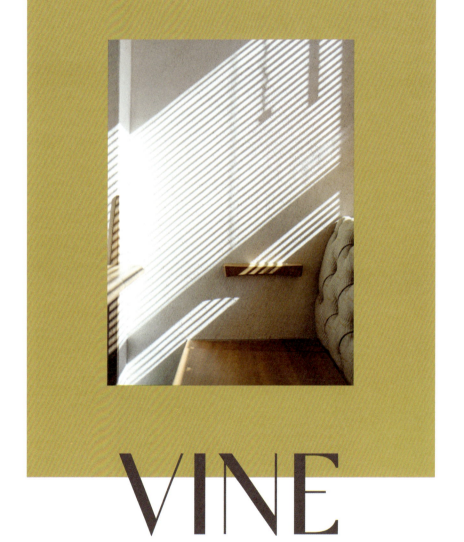

DAY 25

WEEK 04

VINE

John 15

[1] "I am the true vine, and my Father is the gardener. [2] Every branch in me that does not produce fruit he removes, and he prunes every branch that produces fruit so that it will produce more fruit. [3] You are already clean because of the word I have spoken to you. [4] Remain in me, and I in you. Just as a branch is unable to produce fruit by itself unless it remains on the vine, neither can you unless you remain in me.

[5] I am the vine; you are the branches.

The one who remains in me and I in him produces much fruit, because you can do nothing without me. [6] If anyone does not remain in me, he is thrown aside like a branch and he withers. They gather them, throw them into the fire, and they are burned. [7] If you remain in me and my words remain in you, ask whatever you want and it will be done for you. [8] My Father is glorified by this: that you produce much fruit and prove to be my disciples.

CHRISTLIKE LOVE

[9] "As the Father has loved me, I have also loved you. Remain in my love. [10] If you keep my commands you will remain in my love, just as I have kept my Father's commands and remain in his love.

[11] "I have told you these things so that my joy may be in you and your joy may be complete.

[12] "This is my command: Love one another as I have loved you. [13] No one has greater love than this: to lay down his life for his friends. [14] You are my friends if you do what I command you. [15] I do not call you servants anymore, because a

servant doesn't know what his master is doing. I have called you friends, because I have made known to you everything I have heard from my Father. [16] You did not choose me, but I chose you. I appointed you to go and produce fruit and that your fruit should remain, so that whatever you ask the Father in my name, he will give you.

[17] "This is what I command you: Love one another.

PERSECUTIONS PREDICTED

[18] "If the world hates you, understand that it hated me before it hated you. [19] If you were of the world, the world would love you as its own. However, because you are not of the world, but I have chosen you out of it, the world hates you. [20] Remember the word I spoke to you: 'A servant is not greater than his master.' If they persecuted me, they will also persecute you. If they kept my word, they will also keep yours. [21] But they will do all these things to you on account of my name, because they don't know the one who sent me. [22] If I had not come and spoken to them, they would not be guilty of sin. Now they have no excuse for their sin. [23] The one who hates me also hates my Father. [24] If I had not done the works among them that no one else has done, they would not be guilty of sin. Now they have seen and hated both me and my Father. [25] But this happened so that the statement written in their law might be fulfilled: They hated me for no reason.

THE COUNSELOR'S MINISTRY

[26] "When the Counselor comes, the one I will send to you from the Father—the Spirit of truth who proceeds from the Father—he will testify about me. [27] You also will testify, because you have been with me from the beginning."

🔖 GOING DEEPER

Hosea 14:4–8

A PROMISE OF RESTORATION

[4] I will heal their apostasy;
I will freely love them,
for my anger will have turned from him.
[5] I will be like the dew to Israel;
he will blossom like the lily
and take root like the cedars of Lebanon.
[6] His new branches will spread,
and his splendor will be like the olive tree,
his fragrance, like the forest of Lebanon.
[7] The people will return and live beneath his shade.
They will grow grain
and blossom like the vine.
His renown will be like the wine of Lebanon.

[8] Ephraim, why should I have anything more
to do with idols?
It is I who answer and watch over him.
I am like a flourishing pine tree;
your fruit comes from me.

Philippians 1:9–11

[9] And I pray this: that your love will keep on growing in knowledge and every kind of discernment, [10] so that you may approve the things that are superior and may be pure and blameless in the day of Christ, [11] filled with the fruit of righteousness that comes through Jesus Christ to the glory and praise of God.

People who interacted with Jesus:	*How they responded to Him:*	*How He engaged with them:*

In today's reading there was...

(check all that apply)

○ *A miracle*

_____

○ *An "I am" statement*

_____

○ *A festival or feast*

☐ PASSOVER

☐ FESTIVAL OF TABERNACLES

☐ FESTIVAL OF DEDICATION

☐ OTHER _____

Descriptive details I noticed:

Statements about Jesus's identity:	*Statements about Jesus's mission:*

JESUS PROMISES THE SPIRIT

WEEK 04

"IT IS FOR YOUR BENEFIT THAT I GO AWAY, BECAUSE IF I DON'T GO AWAY THE COUNSELOR WILL NOT COME TO YOU." —JOHN 16:7

John 16

¹ "I have told you these things to keep you from stumbling. ² They will ban you from the synagogues. In fact, a time is coming when anyone who kills you will think he is offering service to God. ³ They will do these things because they haven't known the Father or me. ⁴ But I have told you these things so that when their time comes you will remember I told them to you. I didn't tell you these things from the beginning, because I was with you. ⁵ But now I am going away to him who sent me, and not one of you asks me, 'Where are you going?' ⁶ Yet, because I have spoken these things to you, sorrow has filled your heart. ⁷ Nevertheless, I am telling you the truth. It is for your benefit that I go away, because if I don't go away the Counselor will not come to you. If I go, I will send him to you. ⁸ When he comes, he will convict the world about sin, righteousness, and judgment: ⁹ About sin, because they do not believe in me; ¹⁰ about righteousness, because I am going to the Father and you will no longer see me; ¹¹ and about judgment, because the ruler of this world has been judged.

¹² "I still have many things to tell you, but you can't bear them now.

¹³ When the Spirit of truth comes, he will guide you into all the truth.

For he will not speak on his own, but he will speak whatever he hears. He will also declare to you what is to come. ¹⁴ He will glorify me, because he will take from what is mine and declare it to you. ¹⁵ Everything the Father has is mine. This is why I told you that he takes from what is mine and will declare it to you.

SORROW TURNED TO JOY

¹⁶ "In a little while, you will no longer see me; again in a little while, you will see me."

¹⁷ Then some of his disciples said to one another, "What is this he's telling us: 'In a little while, you will not see me; again in a little while, you will see me,' and, 'Because I am going to the Father'?" ¹⁸ They said, "What is this he is saying, 'In a little while'? We don't know what he's talking about."

¹⁹ Jesus knew they wanted to ask him, and so he said to them, "Are you asking one another about what I said, 'In a little while, you will not see me; again in a little while, you will see me'? ²⁰ Truly I tell you, you will weep and mourn, but the world will rejoice. You will become sorrowful, but your sorrow will turn to joy. ²¹ When a woman is in labor, she has pain because her time has come. But when she has given birth to a child, she no longer remembers the suffering because of the joy that a person has been born into the world. ²² So you also have sorrow now. But I will see you again. Your hearts will rejoice, and no one will take away your joy from you.

²³ "In that day you will not ask me anything. Truly I tell you, anything you ask the Father in my name, he will give you. ²⁴ Until now you have asked for nothing in my name. Ask and you will receive, so that your joy may be complete.

JESUS THE VICTOR

²⁵ "I have spoken these things to you in figures of speech. A time is coming when I will no longer speak to you in figures, but I will tell you plainly about the Father. ²⁶ On that day you will ask in my name, and I am not telling you that I will ask the Father on your behalf. ²⁷ For the Father himself loves you, because you have loved me and have believed that I came from God. ²⁸ I came from the Father and have come into the world. Again, I am leaving the world and going to the Father."

²⁹ His disciples said, "Look, now you're speaking plainly and not using any figurative language. ³⁰ Now we know that you know everything and don't need anyone to question you. By this we believe that you came from God."

³¹ Jesus responded to them, "Do you now believe? ³² Indeed, an hour is coming, and has come, when each of you will be scattered to his own home, and you will leave me alone. Yet I am not alone, because the Father is with me. ³³ I have told you these things so that in me you may have peace. You will have suffering in this world. Be courageous! I have conquered the world."

GOING DEEPER

Isaiah 32:14–18

¹⁴ For the palace will be deserted,
the busy city abandoned.
The hill and the watchtower will become
barren places forever,
the joy of wild donkeys,
and a pasture for flocks,

¹⁵ until the Spirit from on high is poured out on us.
Then the desert will become an orchard,
and the orchard will seem like a forest.
¹⁶ Then justice will inhabit the wilderness,
and righteousness will dwell in the orchard.

¹⁷ The result of righteousness will be peace;
the effect of righteousness
will be quiet confidence forever.
¹⁸ Then my people will dwell in a peaceful place,
in safe and secure dwellings.

Joel 2:28–29

GOD'S PROMISE OF HIS SPIRIT

²⁸ "After this
I will pour out my Spirit on all humanity;
then your sons and your daughters will prophesy,
your old men will have dreams,
and your young men will see visions.
²⁹ I will even pour out my Spirit
on the male and female slaves in those days."

Romans 8:12–17

THE HOLY SPIRIT'S MINISTRIES

¹² So then, brothers and sisters, we are not obligated to the flesh to live according to the flesh, ¹³ because if you live according to the flesh, you are going to die. But if by the Spirit you put to death the deeds of the body, you will live. ¹⁴ For all those led by God's Spirit are God's sons. ¹⁵ For you did not receive a spirit of slavery to fall back into fear. Instead, you received the Spirit of adoption, by whom we cry out, "*Abba*, Father!" ¹⁶ The Spirit himself testifies together with our spirit that we are God's children, ¹⁷ and if children, also heirs—heirs of God and coheirs with Christ—if indeed we suffer with him so that we may also be glorified with him.

People who interacted with Jesus:	How they responded to Him:	How He engaged with them:

In today's reading there was...

(check all that apply)

○ *A miracle*

_____

○ *An "I am" statement*

_____

○ *A festival or feast*

☐ PASSOVER

☐ FESTIVAL OF TABERNACLES

☐ FESTIVAL OF DEDICATION

☐ OTHER _____

Descriptive details I noticed:

Statements about Jesus's identity:	Statements about Jesus's mission:

GRACE

DAY

Take this day
to catch up on
your reading,
pray, and rest in
the presence
of the Lord.

"This is my servant;
I strengthen him,
this is my chosen
one; I delight in him.
I have put my
Spirit on him;
he will bring justice
to the nations."

ISAIAH 42:1

WEEKLY

*Scripture is God breathed and true.
When we memorize it, we carry the good
news of Jesus with us wherever we go.*

This week we will memorize John 1:4–5.
Here John continues to draw on the
themes of the creation narrative, pointing
to Jesus as the source of both life and light.
Throughout the Gospels we see Jesus not
only identify Himself using these terms,
but fulfill them with the actions of His
ministry (Jn 8:12; 11:25). Jesus is the light
that has overcome the darkness.

TRUTH

In the beginning was the Word, and the Word was with God, and the Word was God. He was with God in the beginning. All things were created through him, and apart from him not one thing was created that has been created. In him was life, and that life was the light of men. That light shines in the darkness, and yet the darkness did not overcome it.

JOHN 1:1–5

See tips for memorizing Scripture on page 164.

WEEK

THE GLORIFIED ONE

05

John 17

JESUS PRAYS FOR HIMSELF

[1] Jesus spoke these things, looked up to heaven, and said, "Father, the hour has come. Glorify your Son so that the Son may glorify you, [2] since you gave him authority over all people, so that he may give eternal life to everyone you have given him. [3] This is eternal life: that they may know you, the only true God, and the one you have sent—Jesus Christ. [4] I have glorified you on the earth by completing the work you gave me to do. [5] Now, Father, glorify me in your presence with that glory I had with you before the world existed.

JESUS PRAYS FOR HIS DISCIPLES

[6] "I have revealed your name to the people you gave me from the world. They were yours, you gave them to me, and they have kept your word. [7] Now they know that everything you have given me is from you, [8] because I have given them the words you gave me. They have received them and have known for certain that I came from you. They have believed that you sent me.

[9] "I pray for them. I am not praying for the world but for those you have given me, because they are yours. [10] Everything I have is yours, and everything you have is mine, and I am glorified in them. [11] I am no longer in the world, but they are in the world, and I am coming to you. Holy Father, protect them by your name that you have given me, so that they may be one as we are one. [12] While I was with them, I was protecting them by your name that you have given me. I guarded them and not one of them is lost, except the son of destruction, so that the Scripture may be fulfilled. [13] Now I am coming to you, and I speak these things in the world so that they may have my joy completed in them. [14] I have given them your word. The world hated them because they are not of the world, just as I am not of the world. [15] I am not praying that you take them out of the world but that you protect them from the evil one. [16] They are not of the world, just as I am not of the world. [17] Sanctify them by the truth; your word is truth. [18] As you sent me into the world, I also have sent them into the world. [19] I sanctify myself for them, so that they also may be sanctified by the truth.

²⁰ "I pray not only for these, but also for those who believe in me through their word.

²¹ May they all be one, as you, Father, are in me and I am in you.

May they also be in us, so that the world may believe you sent me. ²² I have given them the glory you have given me, so that they may be one as we are one. ²³ I am in them and you are in me, so that they may be made completely one, that the world may know you have sent me and have loved them as you have loved me.

²⁴ "Father, I want those you have given me to be with me where I am, so that they will see my glory, which you have given me because you loved me before the world's foundation. ²⁵ Righteous Father, the world has not known you. However, I have known you, and they have known that you sent me. ²⁶ I made your name known to them and will continue to make it known, so that the love you have loved me with may be in them and I may be in them."

GOING DEEPER

Isaiah 42:8

"I am the Lord. That is my name,
and I will not give my glory to another
or my praise to idols."

1 John 5:20

And we know that the Son of God has come and has given us understanding so that we may know the true one. We are in the true one—that is, in his Son, Jesus Christ. He is the true God and eternal life.

People who interacted with Jesus:	How they responded to Him:	How He engaged with them:

In today's reading there was...

(check all that apply)

○ A miracle

_____

○ An "I am" statement

_____

○ A festival or feast

☐ PASSOVER

☐ FESTIVAL OF TABERNACLES

☐ FESTIVAL OF DEDICATION

☐ OTHER _____

Descriptive details I noticed:

Statements about Jesus's identity:	Statements about Jesus's mission:

JESUS TESTIFIES ABOUT HIS KINGDOM

WEEK 05

John 18

JESUS BETRAYED

¹ After Jesus had said these things, he went out with his disciples across the Kidron Valley, where there was a garden, and he and his disciples went into it. ² Judas, who betrayed him, also knew the place, because Jesus often met there with his disciples. ³ So Judas took a company of soldiers and some officials from the chief priests and the Pharisees and came there with lanterns, torches, and weapons.

⁴ Then Jesus, knowing everything that was about to happen to him, went out and said to them, "Who is it that you're seeking?"

⁵ "Jesus of Nazareth," they answered.

"I am he," Jesus told them.

Judas, who betrayed him, was also standing with them. ⁶ When Jesus told them, "I am he," they stepped back and fell to the ground.

⁷ Then he asked them again, "Who is it that you're seeking?"

"Jesus of Nazareth," they said.

⁸ "I told you I am he," Jesus replied. "So if you're looking for me, let these men go." ⁹ This was to fulfill the words he had said: "I have not lost one of those you have given me."

¹⁰ Then Simon Peter, who had a sword, drew it, struck the high priest's servant, and cut off his right ear. (The servant's name was Malchus.)

¹¹ At that, Jesus said to Peter, "Put your sword away! Am I not to drink the cup the Father has given me?"

JESUS ARRESTED AND TAKEN TO ANNAS

¹² Then the company of soldiers, the commander, and the Jewish officials arrested Jesus and tied him up. ¹³ First they led him to Annas, since he was the father-in-law of Caiaphas, who was high priest that year. ¹⁴ Caiaphas was the one who had advised the Jews that it would be better for one man to die for the people.

PETER DENIES JESUS

¹⁵ Simon Peter was following Jesus, as was another disciple. That disciple was an acquaintance of the high priest; so he went with Jesus into the high priest's courtyard. ¹⁶ But Peter remained standing outside by the door. So the other disciple, the one known to the high priest, went out and spoke to the girl who was the doorkeeper and brought Peter in.

¹⁷ Then the servant girl who was the doorkeeper said to Peter, "You aren't one of this man's disciples too, are you?"

"I am not," he said. ¹⁸ Now the servants and the officials had made a charcoal fire, because it was cold. They were standing there warming themselves, and Peter was standing with them, warming himself.

JESUS BEFORE ANNAS

¹⁹ The high priest questioned Jesus about his disciples and about his teaching.

²⁰ "I have spoken openly to the world," Jesus answered him. "I have always taught in the synagogue and in the temple, where all the Jews gather, and I haven't spoken anything in secret. ²¹ Why do you question me? Question those who heard what I told them. Look, they know what I said."

²² When he had said these things, one of the officials standing by slapped Jesus, saying, "Is this the way you answer the high priest?"

²³ "If I have spoken wrongly," Jesus answered him, "give evidence about the wrong; but if rightly, why do you hit me?" ²⁴ Then Annas sent him bound to Caiaphas the high priest.

PETER DENIES JESUS TWICE MORE

²⁵ Now Simon Peter was standing and warming himself. They said to him, "You aren't one of his disciples too, are you?"

He denied it and said, "I am not."

²⁶ One of the high priest's servants, a relative of the man whose ear Peter had cut off, said, "Didn't I see you with him in the garden?" ²⁷ Peter denied it again. Immediately a rooster crowed.

JESUS BEFORE PILATE

²⁸ Then they led Jesus from Caiaphas to the governor's headquarters. It was early morning. They did not enter the headquarters themselves; otherwise they would be defiled and unable to eat the Passover.

²⁹ So Pilate came out to them and said, "What charge do you bring against this man?"

³⁰ They answered him, "If this man weren't a criminal, we wouldn't have handed him over to you."

³¹ Pilate told them, "You take him and judge him according to your law."

"It's not legal for us to put anyone to death," the Jews declared. ³² They said this so that Jesus's words might be fulfilled indicating what kind of death he was going to die.

³³ Then Pilate went back into the headquarters, summoned Jesus, and said to him, "Are you the king of the Jews?"

³⁴ Jesus answered, "Are you asking this on your own, or have others told you about me?"

³⁵ "I'm not a Jew, am I?" Pilate replied. "Your own nation and the chief priests handed you over to me. What have you done?"

³⁶ "My kingdom is not of this world," said Jesus. "If my kingdom were of this world, my servants would fight, so that I wouldn't be handed over to the Jews. But as it is, my kingdom is not from here."

³⁷ "You are a king then?" Pilate asked.

"You say that I'm a king," Jesus replied.

"I was born for this, and I have come into the world for this: to testify to the truth.

Everyone who is of the truth listens to my voice."

[38] "What is truth?" said Pilate.

JESUS OR BARABBAS

After he had said this, he went out to the Jews again and told them, "I find no grounds for charging him. [39] You have a custom that I release one prisoner to you at the Passover. So, do you want me to release to you the king of the Jews?"

[40] They shouted back, "Not this man, but Barabbas!" Now Barabbas was a revolutionary.

⬥ GOING DEEPER

Isaiah 9:2–7

[2] The people walking in darkness
have seen a great light;
a light has dawned
on those living in the land of darkness.
[3] You have enlarged the nation
and increased its joy.
The people have rejoiced before you
as they rejoice at harvest time
and as they rejoice when dividing spoils.
[4] For you have shattered their oppressive yoke
and the rod on their shoulders,
the staff of their oppressor,
just as you did on the day of Midian.
[5] For every trampling boot of battle
and the bloodied garments of war
will be burned as fuel for the fire.
[6] For a child will be born for us,
a son will be given to us,
and the government will be on his shoulders.
He will be named
Wonderful Counselor, Mighty God,
Eternal Father, Prince of Peace.
[7] The dominion will be vast,
and its prosperity will never end.
He will reign on the throne of David
and over his kingdom,
to establish and sustain it
with justice and righteousness from now on and forever.
The zeal of the LORD of Armies will accomplish this.

Daniel 7:14

He was given dominion
and glory and a kingdom,
so that those of every people,
nation, and language
should serve him.

His dominion is an
everlasting dominion
that will not pass away,
and his kingdom is one
that will not be destroyed.

People who interacted with Jesus:	How they responded to Him:	How He engaged with them:

In today's reading there was...

(check all that apply)

○ A miracle

_____

○ An "I am" statement

_____

○ A festival or feast

☐ PASSOVER

☐ FESTIVAL OF TABERNACLES

☐ FESTIVAL OF DEDICATION

☐ OTHER _____

Descriptive details I noticed:

Statements about Jesus's identity:	Statements about Jesus's mission:

BLESSED REDEEMER

WORDS | AVIS B. CHRISTIANSEN
MUSIC | HARRY DIXON LOES

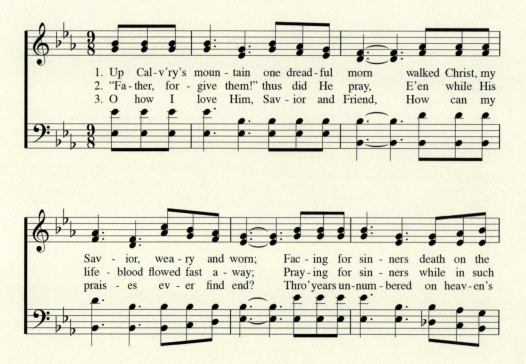

1. Up Cal-v'ry's moun-tain one dread-ful morn walked Christ, my
2. "Fa-ther, for-give them!" thus did He pray, E'en while His
3. O how I love Him, Sav-ior and Friend, How can my

Sav-ior, wea-ry and worn; Fac-ing for sin-ners death on the
life-blood flowed fast a-way; Pray-ing for sin-ners while in such
prais-es ev-er find end? Thro' years un-num-bered on heav-en's

cross,   That He might save them from end-less loss.
woe—   no one but Je-sus ev-er loved so.
shore,   My tongue shall praise Him for-ev-er-more.

Chorus

Bless-ed Re-deem-er! Pre-cious Re-deem-er! Seems now I

see Him on Cal-va-ry's tree; Wound-ed and bleed-ing, for sin-ners

plead-ing— blind and un-heed-ing— dy-ing for me!

THE INNOCENT ONE IS CRUCIFIED

WEEK 05

JESUS FLOGGED AND MOCKED

[1] Then Pilate took Jesus and had him flogged. [2] The soldiers also twisted together a crown of thorns, put it on his head, and clothed him in a purple robe. [3] And they kept coming up to him and saying, "Hail, king of the Jews!" and were slapping his face.

[4] Pilate went outside again and said to them, "Look, I'm bringing him out to you to let you know I find no grounds for charging him." [5] Then Jesus came out wearing the crown of thorns and the purple robe. Pilate said to them, "Here is the man!"

PILATE SENTENCES JESUS TO DEATH

[6] When the chief priests and the temple servants saw him, they shouted, "Crucify! Crucify!"

Pilate responded, "Take him and crucify him yourselves, since I find no grounds for charging him."

[7] "We have a law," the Jews replied to him, "and according to that law he ought to die, because he made himself the Son of God."

[8] When Pilate heard this statement, he was more afraid than ever. [9] He went back into the headquarters and asked Jesus, "Where are you from?" But Jesus did not give him an answer. [10] So Pilate said to him, "Do you refuse to speak to me? Don't you know that I have the authority to release you and the authority to crucify you?"

[11] "You would have no authority over me at all," Jesus answered him, "if it hadn't been given you from above. This is why the one who handed me over to you has the greater sin."

[12] From that moment Pilate kept trying to release him. But the Jews shouted, "If you release this man, you are not Caesar's friend. Anyone who makes himself a king opposes Caesar!"

[13] When Pilate heard these words, he brought Jesus outside. He sat down on the judge's seat in a place called the Stone Pavement (but in Aramaic, *Gabbatha*). [14] It was the preparation day for the Passover, and it was about noon. Then he told the Jews, "Here is your king!"

[15] They shouted, "Take him away! Take him away! Crucify him!"

Pilate said to them, "Should I crucify your king?"

"We have no king but Caesar!" the chief priests answered.

[16] Then he handed him over to be crucified.

THE CRUCIFIXION

Then they took Jesus away. [17] Carrying the cross by himself, he went out to what is called Place of the Skull, which in Aramaic is called *Golgotha*. [18] There they crucified him and two others with him, one on either side, with Jesus in the middle. [19] Pilate also had a sign made and put on the cross. It said: JESUS OF NAZARETH, THE KING OF THE JEWS. [20] Many of the Jews read this sign, because the place where Jesus was crucified was near the city, and it was written in Aramaic, Latin, and Greek. [21] So the chief priests of the Jews said to Pilate, "Don't write, 'The king of the Jews,' but that he said, 'I am the king of the Jews.'"

[22] Pilate replied, "What I have written, I have written."

[23] When the soldiers crucified Jesus, they took his clothes and divided them into four parts, a part for each soldier. They also took the tunic, which was seamless, woven in one piece from the top. [24] So they said to one another, "Let's not tear it, but cast lots for it, to see who gets it." This happened that the Scripture might be fulfilled that says: They divided my clothes among themselves, and they cast lots for my clothing. This is what the soldiers did.

JESUS'S PROVISION FOR HIS MOTHER

[25] Standing by the cross of Jesus were his mother, his mother's sister, Mary the wife of Clopas, and Mary Magdalene. [26] When Jesus saw his mother and the disciple he loved

standing there, he said to his mother, "Woman, here is your son." [27] Then he said to the disciple, "Here is your mother." And from that hour the disciple took her into his home.

THE FINISHED WORK OF JESUS

[28] After this, when Jesus knew that everything was now finished that the Scripture might be fulfilled, he said, "I'm thirsty." [29] A jar full of sour wine was sitting there; so they fixed a sponge full of sour wine on a hyssop branch and held it up to his mouth.

[30] When Jesus had received the sour wine, he said, "It is finished." Then bowing his head, he gave up his spirit.

JESUS'S SIDE PIERCED

[31] Since it was the preparation day, the Jews did not want the bodies to remain on the cross on the Sabbath (for that Sabbath was a special day). They requested that Pilate have the men's legs broken and that their bodies be taken away. [32] So the soldiers came and broke the legs of the first man and of the other one who had been crucified with him. [33] When they came to Jesus, they did not break his legs since they saw that he was already dead. [34] But one of the soldiers pierced his side with a spear, and at once blood and water came out. [35] He who saw this has testified so that you also may believe. His testimony is true, and he knows he is telling the truth. [36] For these things happened so that the Scripture would be fulfilled: Not one of his bones will be broken. [37] Also, another Scripture says: They will look at the one they pierced.

JESUS'S BURIAL

[38] After this, Joseph of Arimathea, who was a disciple of Jesus—but secretly because of his fear of the Jews—asked Pilate that he might remove Jesus's body. Pilate gave him permission; so he came and took his body away. [39] Nicodemus (who had previously come to him at night) also came, bringing a mixture of about seventy-five pounds of myrrh and aloes. [40] They took Jesus's body and wrapped it in linen cloths with the fragrant spices, according to the burial custom of the Jews. [41] There was a garden in the place where he was crucified. A new tomb was in the garden; no one had yet been placed in it. [42] They placed Jesus there because of the Jewish day of preparation and since the tomb was nearby.

Psalm 22:1–8

FROM SUFFERING TO PRAISE

For the choir director: according to "The Deer of the Dawn." A psalm of David.

[1] My God, my God, why have you abandoned me?
Why are you so far from my deliverance
and from my words of groaning?
[2] My God, I cry by day, but you do not answer,
by night, yet I have no rest.
[3] But you are holy,
enthroned on the praises of Israel.
[4] Our ancestors trusted in you;
they trusted, and you rescued them.
[5] They cried to you and were set free;
they trusted in you and were not disgraced.

[6] But I am a worm and not a man,
scorned by mankind and despised by people.
[7] Everyone who sees me mocks me;
they sneer and shake their heads:
[8] "He relies on the Lord;
let him save him;
let the Lord rescue him,
since he takes pleasure in him."

1 Peter 2:22–25

[22] He did not commit sin, and no deceit was found in his mouth; [23] when he was insulted, he did not insult in return; when he suffered, he did not threaten but entrusted himself to the one who judges justly. [24] He himself bore our sins in his body on the tree; so that, having died to sins, we might live for righteousness. By his wounds you have been healed. [25] For you were like sheep going astray, but you have now returned to the Shepherd and Overseer of your souls.

People who interacted with Jesus:	How they responded to Him:	How He engaged with them:

In today's reading there was...
(check all that apply)

○ A miracle

_____

○ An "I am" statement

_____

○ A festival or feast

☐ PASSOVER

☐ FESTIVAL OF TABERNACLES

☐ FESTIVAL OF DEDICATION

☐ OTHER _____

Descriptive details I noticed:

Statements about Jesus's identity:	Statements about Jesus's mission:

THE RISEN

ONE

John 20

THE EMPTY TOMB

¹ On the first day of the week Mary Magdalene came to the tomb early, while it was still dark. She saw that the stone had been removed from the tomb. ² So she went running to Simon Peter and to the other disciple, the one Jesus loved, and said to them, "They've taken the Lord out of the tomb, and we don't know where they've put him!"

³ At that, Peter and the other disciple went out, heading for the tomb. ⁴ The two were running together, but the other disciple outran Peter and got to the tomb first. ⁵ Stooping down, he saw the linen cloths lying there, but he did not go in. ⁶ Then, following him, Simon Peter also came. He entered the tomb and saw the linen cloths lying there. ⁷ The wrapping that had been on his head was not lying with the linen cloths but was folded up in a separate place by itself. ⁸ The other disciple, who had reached the tomb first, then also went in, saw, and believed.

⁹ For they did not yet understand the Scripture that he must rise from the dead.

¹⁰ Then the disciples returned to the place where they were staying.

MARY MAGDALENE SEES THE RISEN LORD

¹¹ But Mary stood outside the tomb, crying. As she was crying, she stooped to look into the tomb. ¹² She saw two angels in white sitting where Jesus's body had been lying, one at the head and the other at the feet. ¹³ They said to her, "Woman, why are you crying?"

"Because they've taken away my Lord," she told them, "and I don't know where they've put him."

¹⁴ Having said this, she turned around and saw Jesus standing there, but she did not know it was Jesus. ¹⁵ "Woman," Jesus said to her, "why are you crying? Who is it that you're seeking?"

Supposing he was the gardener, she replied, "Sir, if you've carried him away, tell me where you've put him, and I will take him away."

¹⁶ Jesus said to her, "Mary."

Turning around, she said to him in Aramaic, *"Rabboni!"*—which means "Teacher."

¹⁷ "Don't cling to me," Jesus told her, "since I have not yet ascended to the Father. But go to my brothers and tell them that I am ascending to my Father and your Father, to my God and your God."

¹⁸ Mary Magdalene went and announced to the disciples, "I have seen the Lord!" And she told them what he had said to her.

THE DISCIPLES COMMISSIONED

¹⁹ When it was evening on that first day of the week, the disciples were gathered together with the doors locked because they feared the Jews. Jesus came, stood among them, and said to them, "Peace be with you."

²⁰ Having said this, he showed them his hands and his side. So the disciples rejoiced when they saw the Lord.

²¹ Jesus said to them again, "Peace be with you. As the Father has sent me, I also send you." ²² After saying this, he breathed on them and said, "Receive the Holy Spirit. ²³ If you forgive the sins of any, they are forgiven them; if you retain the sins of any, they are retained."

THOMAS SEES AND BELIEVES

²⁴ But Thomas (called "Twin"), one of the Twelve, was not with them when Jesus came. ²⁵ So the other disciples were telling him, "We've seen the Lord!"

But he said to them, "If I don't see the mark of the nails in his hands, put my finger into the mark of the nails, and put my hand into his side, I will never believe."

26 A week later his disciples were indoors again, and Thomas was with them. Even though the doors were locked, Jesus came and stood among them and said, "Peace be with you."

27 Then he said to Thomas, "Put your finger here and look at my hands. Reach out your hand and put it into my side. Don't be faithless, but believe."

28 Thomas responded to him, "My Lord and my God!"

29 Jesus said, "Because you have seen me, you have believed. Blessed are those who have not seen and yet believe."

THE PURPOSE OF THIS GOSPEL

30 Jesus performed many other signs in the presence of his disciples that are not written in this book. 31 But these are written so that you may believe that Jesus is the Messiah, the Son of God, and that by believing you may have life in his name.

🌿 GOING DEEPER

Daniel 10:5–6

5 I looked up, and there was a man dressed in linen, with a belt of gold from Uphaz around his waist. 6 His body was like beryl, his face like the brilliance of lightning, his eyes like flaming torches, his arms and feet like the gleam of polished bronze, and the sound of his words like the sound of a multitude.

Acts 2:24–32

24 God raised him up, ending the pains of death, because it was not possible for him to be held by death. 25 For David says of him:

I saw the Lord ever before me;
because he is at my right hand,
I will not be shaken.
26 Therefore my heart is glad
and my tongue rejoices.
Moreover, my flesh will rest in hope,
27 because you will not abandon me in Hades
or allow your holy one to see decay.
28 You have revealed the paths of life to me;
you will fill me with gladness
in your presence.

29 Brothers and sisters, I can confidently speak to you about the patriarch David: He is both dead and buried, and his tomb is with us to this day. 30 Since he was a prophet, he knew that God had sworn an oath to him to seat one of his descendants on his throne. 31 Seeing what was to come, he spoke concerning the resurrection of the Messiah: He was not abandoned in Hades, and his flesh did not experience decay.

32 God has raised this Jesus; we are all witnesses of this.

People who interacted with Jesus:	How they responded to Him:	How He engaged with them:

In today's reading there was...

(check all that apply)

○ A miracle

_____

○ An "I am" statement

_____

○ A festival or feast

☐ PASSOVER

☐ FESTIVAL OF TABERNACLES

☐ FESTIVAL OF DEDICATION

☐ OTHER _____

Descriptive details I noticed:

Statements about Jesus's identity:	Statements about Jesus's mission:

JESUS'S FINAL INVITATION

John 21

JESUS'S THIRD APPEARANCE TO THE DISCIPLES

¹ After this, Jesus revealed himself again to his disciples by the Sea of Tiberias. He revealed himself in this way:

² Simon Peter, Thomas (called "Twin"), Nathanael from Cana of Galilee, Zebedee's sons, and two others of his disciples were together.

³ "I'm going fishing," Simon Peter said to them.

"We're coming with you," they told him. They went out and got into the boat, but that night they caught nothing.

⁴ When daybreak came, Jesus stood on the shore, but the disciples did not know it was Jesus. ⁵ "Friends," Jesus called to them, "you don't have any fish, do you?"

"No," they answered.

⁶ "Cast the net on the right side of the boat," he told them, "and you'll find some." So they did, and they were unable to haul it in because of the large number of fish. ⁷ The disciple, the one Jesus loved, said to Peter, "It is the Lord!"

When Simon Peter heard that it was the Lord, he tied his outer clothing around him (for he had taken it off) and plunged into the sea. ⁸ Since they were not far from land (about a hundred yards away), the other disciples came in the boat, dragging the net full of fish.

⁹ When they got out on land, they saw a charcoal fire there, with fish lying on it, and bread. ¹⁰ "Bring some of the fish you've just caught," Jesus told them. ¹¹ So Simon Peter climbed up and hauled the net ashore, full of large fish—153 of them. Even though there were so many, the net was not torn.

¹² "Come and have breakfast," Jesus told them. None of the disciples dared ask him, "Who are you?" because they knew it was the Lord. ¹³ Jesus came, took the bread, and gave it to them. He did the same with the fish. ¹⁴ This was now the third time Jesus appeared to the disciples after he was raised from the dead.

[15] When they had eaten breakfast, Jesus asked Simon Peter, "Simon, son of John, do you love me more than these?"

"Yes, Lord," he said to him, "you know that I love you."

"Feed my lambs," he told him. [16] A second time he asked him, "Simon, son of John, do you love me?"

"Yes, Lord," he said to him, "you know that I love you."

"Shepherd my sheep," he told him.

[17] He asked him the third time, "Simon, son of John, do you love me?"

Peter was grieved that he asked him the third time, "Do you love me?" He said, "Lord, you know everything; you know that I love you."

"Feed my sheep," Jesus said. [18] "Truly I tell you, when you were younger, you would tie your belt and walk wherever you wanted. But when you grow old, you will stretch out your hands and someone else will tie you and carry you where you don't want to go." [19] He said this to indicate by what kind of death Peter would glorify God. After saying this, he told him, "Follow me."

CORRECTING A FALSE REPORT

[20] So Peter turned around and saw the disciple Jesus loved following them, the one who had leaned back against Jesus at the supper and asked, "Lord, who is the one that's going to betray you?" [21] When Peter saw him, he said to Jesus, "Lord, what about him?"

[22] "If I want him to remain until I come," Jesus answered, "what is that to you? As for you, follow me."

[23] So this rumor spread to the brothers and sisters that this disciple would not die. Yet Jesus did not tell him that he would not die, but, "If I want him to remain until I come, what is that to you?"

EPILOGUE

[24] This is the disciple who testifies to these things and who wrote them down. We know that his testimony is true.

[25] And there are also many other things that Jesus did, which, if every one of them were written down, I suppose not even the world itself could contain the books that would be written.

GOING DEEPER

Hebrews 2:17–18

[17] Therefore, he had to be like his brothers and sisters in every way, so that he could become a merciful and faithful high priest in matters pertaining to God, to make atonement for the sins of the people. [18] For since he himself has suffered when he was tempted, he is able to help those who are tempted.

1 Peter 5:1–4

ABOUT THE ELDERS

[1] I exhort the elders among you as a fellow elder and witness to the sufferings of Christ, as well as one who shares in the glory about to be revealed: [2] Shepherd God's flock among you, not overseeing out of compulsion but willingly, as God would have you; not out of greed for money but eagerly; [3] not lording it over those entrusted to you, but being examples to the flock. [4] And when the chief Shepherd appears, you will receive the unfading crown of glory.

People who interacted with Jesus:	How they responded to Him:	How He engaged with them:

In today's reading there was...

(check all that apply)

○ A miracle

_____

○ An "I am" statement

_____

○ A festival or feast

☐ PASSOVER

☐ FESTIVAL OF TABERNACLES

☐ FESTIVAL OF DEDICATION

☐ OTHER _____

Descriptive details I noticed:

Statements about Jesus's identity:	Statements about Jesus's mission:

GRACE

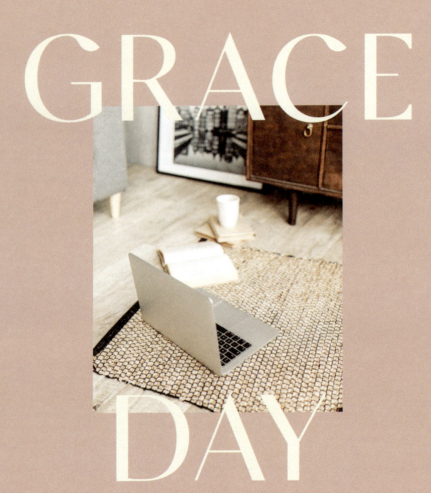

DAY

Take this day
to catch up on
your reading,
pray, and rest in
the presence
of the Lord.

And we know that the Son of God has come and has given us understanding so that we may know the true one. We are in the true one—that is, in his Son, Jesus Christ. He is the true God and eternal life.

1 JOHN 5:20

WEEKLY

Scripture is God breathed and true. When we memorize it, we carry the good news of Jesus with us wherever we go.

Over the past several weeks, we have memorized John 1:1–5. Test your memorization of the passage by filling in the blanks on the following page.

TRUTH

In the beginning was the _____, and the
Word was with ____, and the Word ___
God. He was with God in the _____.
All things were _____ through him, and
_____ from him not one thing was created
that has been created. In him was ___,
and that life was the ____ of men. That
light shines in the darkness, and yet the
darkness did not _____ it.

JOHN 1:1–5

See tips for memorizing Scripture on page 164.

Jesus performed many other signs in the presence of his disciples that are not written in this book. But these are written so that you may believe that Jesus is the Messiah, the Son of God, and that by believing you may have life in his name.

JOHN 20:30–31

Tips for Memorizing Scripture

At She Reads Truth, we believe Scripture memorization is an important discipline in your walk with God. Committing God's Word to memory means we carry it with us and we can minister to others wherever we go. As you approach the Weekly Truth verse in this book, try these memorization tips to see which techniques work best for you!

STUDY IT

Study the passage in its biblical context, and ask yourself a few questions before you begin to memorize it: What does this passage say? What does it mean? How would I say this in my own words? What does it teach me about God? Understanding what the passage means helps you know why it is important to carry it with you wherever you go.

Break the passage into smaller sections, memorizing a phrase at a time.

PRAY IT

Use the passage you are memorizing as a prompt for prayer.

WRITE IT

Dedicate a notebook to Scripture memorization, and write the passage over and over again.

Diagram the passage after you write it out. Place a square around the verbs, underline the nouns, and circle any adjectives or adverbs. Say the passage aloud several times, emphasizing the verbs as you repeat it. Then do the same thing again with the nouns, then the adjectives and adverbs.

Write out the first letter of each word in the passage somewhere you can reference it throughout the week as you work on your memorization.

Use a whiteboard to write out the passage. Erase a few words at a time as you continue to repeat it aloud. Keep erasing parts of the passage until you have it all committed to memory.

CREATE

If you can, make up a tune for the passage to sing as you go about your day, or try singing it to the tune of a favorite song.

Sketch the passage, visualizing what each phrase would look like in the form of a picture. Or try using calligraphy or altering the style of your handwriting as you write it out.

Use hand signals or signs to come up with associations for each word or phrase, and repeat the movements as you practice.

SAY IT

Repeat the passage out loud to yourself as you are going through the rhythm of your day—getting ready, pouring your coffee, waiting in traffic, or making dinner.

Listen to the passage read aloud to you.

Record a voice memo on your phone, and listen to it throughout the day, or play it on an audio Bible.

SHARE IT

Memorize the passage with a friend, family member, or mentor. Spontaneously challenge each other to recite the passage, or pick a time to review your passage and practice saying it from memory together.

Send the passage as an encouraging text to a friend, testing yourself as you type to see how much you have memorized so far.

KEEP AT IT!

Set reminders on your phone to prompt you to practice your passage.

Purchase a She Reads Truth Scripture Card Set, or keep a stack of note cards with Scripture you are memorizing by your bed. Practice reciting what you've memorized previously before you go to sleep, ending with the passages you are currently learning. If you wake up in the middle of the night, review them again instead of grabbing your phone. Read them out loud before you get out of bed in the morning.

CSB BOOK ABBREVIATIONS

OLD TESTAMENT

GN Genesis	**JB** Job	**HAB** Habakkuk	**PHP** Philippians
EX Exodus	**PS** Psalms	**ZPH** Zephaniah	**COL** Colossians
LV Leviticus	**PR** Proverbs	**HG** Haggai	**1TH** 1 Thessalonians
NM Numbers	**EC** Ecclesiastes	**ZCH** Zechariah	**2TH** 2 Thessalonians
DT Deuteronomy	**SG** Song of Solomon	**MAL** Malachi	**1TM** 1 Timothy
JOS Joshua	**IS** Isaiah		**2TM** 2 Timothy
JDG Judges	**JR** Jeremiah	NEW TESTAMENT	**TI** Titus
RU Ruth	**LM** Lamentations	**MT** Matthew	**PHM** Philemon
1SM 1 Samuel	**EZK** Ezekiel	**MK** Mark	**HEB** Hebrews
2SM 2 Samuel	**DN** Daniel	**LK** Luke	**JMS** James
1KG 1 Kings	**HS** Hosea	**JN** John	**1PT** 1 Peter
2KG 2 Kings	**JL** Joel	**AC** Acts	**2PT** 2 Peter
1CH 1 Chronicles	**AM** Amos	**RM** Romans	**1JN** 1 John
2CH 2 Chronicles	**OB** Obadiah	**1CO** 1 Corinthians	**2JN** 2 John
EZR Ezra	**JNH** Jonah	**2CO** 2 Corinthians	**3JN** 3 John
NEH Nehemiah	**MC** Micah	**GL** Galatians	**JD** Jude
EST Esther	**NAH** Nahum	**EPH** Ephesians	**RV** Revelation

BIBLIOGRAPHY

Blum, Edwin A., and Trevin Wax, eds. *CSB Study Bible: Notes.* Holman Bible Publishers, 2017.

You just spent 35 days in the Word of God!

MY FAVORITE DAY OF
THIS READING PLAN:

HOW DID I FIND DELIGHT IN GOD'S WORD?

ONE THING I LEARNED
ABOUT GOD:

WHAT WAS GOD DOING IN
MY LIFE DURING THIS STUDY?

WHAT DID I LEARN THAT I WANT TO SHARE
WITH SOMEONE ELSE?

A SPECIFIC PASSAGE OR VERSE
THAT ENCOURAGED ME:

A SPECIFIC PASSAGE OR VERSE THAT
CHALLENGED AND CONVICTED ME: